THE
NANNY
MANUAL

THE NANNY MANUAL

How to Choose and Nurture the Perfect Childcare Partner for Your Family

ALYCE DESROSIERS

Chirp Publishing
San Francisco, CA

© 2018 by Chirp Publishing

Chirp Publishing will donate all proceeds from this book to The Institute for Families and Nannies.

The Institute for Families and Nannies (TIFFAN) is a nonprofit organization providing professional development, education and support to nannies, research and advocacy to professionalize the nanny industry. TIFFAN's activities are supported by philanthropic contributions from individuals and institutions. For more information, visit www.tiffan.org

The Institute for Families and Nannies
San Francisco, California

All efforts have been made by the author and publisher to accurately attribute ideas and quotations. We sincerely apologize for inadvertent errors or omissions.

Editors: Elaine Cummings, Leslie Patrick, Lisa Wolfe
Book Designer: Torre DeRoche
Project Manager: Karla Olson

Print ISBN: 978-0-9815773-0-2
Ebook ISBN: 978-0-9815773-1-9

Library of Congress Control Number: 2017956480

Library of Congress Cataloging-in-Publication Data to come

First Edition

Printed in the United States of America

Dedicated to

My loving partner, Michael Katz

*And in loving memory of my mother, Jean Desrosiers
who passed away while this book was being written*

CONTENTS

INTRODUCTION

Randomly patched on a cork bulletin board in front of me were handwritten announcements from nannies looking for jobs. "I love kids. Will love yours." "Hablo español. Necesito trabajo. Trabajo como nanny." "10 years' experience. Great references. $12/hour."

It was 1996, and my friend Samantha had asked me to help her find a nanny for her three-year-old daughter. Samantha had recently moved to San Francisco with her family for medical care after being diagnosed with a high-risk pregnancy in her second trimester. Once here, she was immediately put on bed rest. Her husband relocated but was commuting back to New York weekly for work. They had no family nearby. The questions were obvious. How could Samantha take care of an active three-year-old while on bed rest? How would she do laundry or get dinner on the table? Samantha needed help in her home every day from the time her daughter woke until bed. The only childcare arrangement that made any sense was hiring a nanny.

Samantha asked me to help her out with this critical hire. I thought, "I can do this!" I was a clinical social worker helping families and children at risk for abuse and neglect. I had been on the board of a start-up childcare center; had done federally funded research on how parents manage work and family; had interned at UCSF's Infant Parent Program and Mills College Children's School; and I was the second of nine children. I was passionate about giving kids a good start in life. Was there anyone more qualified than I was to find a nanny for a good friend?

What I didn't know what just how naïve and idealistic I was. Hiring a nanny was not easy. I walked into a market of childcare workers that was—and still is—unlicensed and unregulated. Literally anyone could post a notice on a bulletin board or in the classified pages of a newspaper saying she wanted to take care of children. There was no government agency checking applicants' experience with kids, reviewing their health and safety certifications or running background checks. That responsibility was left to parents or the nanny placement agencies that charged fees most families couldn't afford. Even knowing what basic requirements to expect and how to hire for those was a responsibility that fell on the shoulders of parents needing childcare.

> One of the most irresponsible and negligent acts of the U.S. federal government is the abdication of its responsibility to ensure that nannies are licensed. How is it that we expect parking lot attendants and dog walkers to obtain a license and yet we fail to expect the same of those caring for the most vulnerable in our society?

It was the '90s, ushering in the birth of the internet. The Web was still in its infancy. Getting hired as a nanny meant pounding the pavement and posting flyers where women pushing baby strollers would go. So, I visited Parents Place, a local nonprofit that had converted a small house into a place where moms gathered for parenting classes and to meet each other over coffee. At that time, a growing percentage of mothers were going back to work after maternity leave. They needed childcare. There was a large influx of immigrants in San Francisco from El Salvador, Nicaragua and Ireland. Many were looking to work as nannies. So, in their very narrow entry hall, Parents Place put up a bulletin board for nannies seeking employment and parents looking for nannies. On any given day, the hallway was jammed with women writing down names and phone numbers while jiggling fussy babies on their hips.

I stood among them, emboldened with enthusiasm and clueless about the challenges this uncharted territory would bring.

How was I to know who would be a good nanny? If someone loves children, does that automatically make the person loving and caring? If someone has 10 years' experience, is that 10 years of good experience? How can someone who doesn't speak English have a conversation with a three-year-old or update a mom about what she did all day? How can I know which applicants to call when all I know about them is two lines written on a ragged note on a community bulletin board?

Even though 20 years have passed and nanny online postings now include photos, résumés and reviews, the most basic question remains: Who is this person and can I trust her to care for the most important person in my life?

I took my lead from the other women queued up in the corridor and wrote down names and phone numbers of anyone who sounded reasonable. With 20 names organized neatly on my notepad, feeling quite smug and satisfied with myself, I returned home and started calling. Three hours later, I had left many voicemail messages, talked to a few candidates and gotten a lot of automated responses about numbers no longer in service. Many people I called did not speak English. Others had already found jobs. Some had very little experience. I was left with two candidates who seemed worth meeting. I was deflated and worried. Only two out of 20 met basic requirements? Was I expecting too much?

Over the years, I've learned that approximately 10 percent of the people I hear from in the open market meet basic requirements. Filtering out and screening approximately 40 to 50 candidates just to get four or five for further consideration is time-consuming and stressful, even for the most organized person.

I made several more trips to the bulletin board for names and numbers. I started calling everyone I knew who might know of someone looking for a nanny position. I went to the playground and asked nannies if they had a friend who needed work. In the supermarket, I stopped at the bulletin boards and scanned postings. I carried my "nanny notepad" everywhere I went. I was no longer proud of the organized listings of names and numbers. Pages were now filled with arrows, circles and lines linking names, numbers and comments. By the end of the first week, I had gathered 60 names and was having a hard time keeping straight who was who. Among them were eight names that I highlighted with a yellow marker. These were reasonable possibilities to consider.

Anxiety started to set in. I began questioning my judgment. My list wasn't getting the five-star rating I had anticipated. Were we expecting too much? My friend's checklist of ideal qualities was short: honest, trustworthy, loving, experienced and within budget. Mine was longer. A nanny should have preschool teaching experience, early childhood education, excellent English skills, maturity, patience and a strong work ethic. This surely wasn't too much to ask for in someone taking on such a huge responsibility. Yet after a week of searching, I realized I had to reset expectations. We simply didn't have the time to look for a needle in a haystack.

Listing the ideal qualities and characteristics that comprise a nanny can be a relatively straightforward and easy task. But the nanny market encompasses a range of candidates with varying degrees of characteristics and skills. Prioritizing characteristics that are all-important is challenging. Even more challenging is that hiring for this position requires looking well beyond what a candidate knows or can do. The hire is about who a person is. Nannies create relationships with parents and the kids they care for. Within these relationships, development happens. The importance of this hire compared with the time available to make the decision defies reason. How can you know who a person is after meeting with her for an hour or even spending time together in a trial for a week? How much do you need to know about a nanny to trust her enough to separate from your child knowing the nanny is doing right by you and your child?

My friend and I went through the list of candidates. We reprioritized our list of expectations and made decisions about whom to meet. I met with this short list of candidates to reconfirm our decision and get more detailed work histories. I called references, copied documents and scheduled interviews.

The afternoon of our first interview Samantha was in a pensive mood. Her daughter was busy playing with her blocks nearby. She looked at me with tears in her eyes. "Do we have to do this?" she said. "I never imagined I would have someone I don't even know in my home taking care of my children. I feel completely out of control. I feel like someone is taking something away from me—something that is so essential to who I am and what I do." In the next breath she said, "Why can't you be my nanny?"

That's when I decided to leave my private practice and begin working with families to help them through the process of hiring nannies who fit their needs. For the past 20 years, I've worked with hundreds of families, facilitated numerous workshops with parents about how to do a successful search and created relationships with hundreds of nannies who do the valuable work of caring for other people's children.

And I've never looked back.

I grew up the second in a family of nine children. My father was one of 15; my mother one of five. We lived 15 minutes away from my grandparents' house and 30 minutes away from the French-Catholic church and parish that my grandparents and other French-Canadian immigrants founded. Sunday mornings were spent at church. Most Sunday afternoons, holidays, birthdays and anniversaries we would get together with a varied assortment of cousins, aunts and uncles at my grandparents' house. There would be a minimum of 30 of us, ranging in age from newborn to 70, cramming those small five rooms, eating and catching up on news and family gossip. After mealtime, all the grandchildren would be sent down to the basement to play "out of sight, out of mind." The eldest children, myself included, would be in charge. Changing diapers, feeding hungry kids, settling fights and soothing temper tantrums were part of the deal. At home, it was the same. There was only so much of my mom's love, attention and time to go around. My dad worked two, often three jobs to make ends meet. Taking care of my brothers and sisters was both a necessity and a way for me to get recognition. At family gatherings or gossiping with neighbors, my mom would say, "My Alyce is never any trouble. I can always count on her." But taking care of others was not just my role. I was surrounded by caregiving. My siblings would help. My aunts and uncles would take care of us when my parents needed a break. My grandmother moved in whenever my mom went into the hospital to deliver one of my siblings. Helping was just something "family does." In our large extended family, nobody ever considered asking someone who was "not family" to care for us. We were proudly independent of outside help.

> As families become more mobile and live long distances from each other, the need to depend on nonfamilial support rises. When this support includes hiring a nanny—a complete stranger—for what can be long hours each day, the profound question arises: who is family and who is raising our children?

This book is about how parents and nannies find each other, make decisions to work together and collaborate to raise healthy, well-adjusted children. It's about the process they go through, how they do it and their worries along the way, as well as about the outcome. It's intended to support your developing relationship with your nanny, to give you a road map to get through the entire process and do it successfully.

There are land mines. They come unexpectedly and, at times, often. This book will help you know what they are so when they arise, you will be in familiar territory.

Thousands of parents have gone through their own process and have done so successfully. Thousands more children have had nannies care for them since infancy and have grown to be young adults capable of creating healthy relationships. Many attest to the benefits of having had a nanny as part of their family life. Many of these children, now as teens and young adults, still call their nannies for advice and comfort.

Modern-day families are pioneers in the parenting arena. The vast majority of children live in households where both parents work. These parents need childcare, and many hire nannies.

The Nanny Manual is about their process—and yours.

Through my work and the relationships I've developed with parents and nannies, I've learned a lot about the complex emotional, social, economic and cultural challenges each must navigate to give loving, responsible and well-informed care to young children. *The Nanny Manual* is a result of this experience and provides a practical guide to help you through the process and ensure you make a good hiring decision.

HOW TO USE THIS BOOK

The Nanny Manual is about the importance of the relationship parents and nannies create to ensure the healthy development of the child in their care. It is both a practical and an emotional guide supporting you in your journey to hire the right nanny for your child and you. Each chapter focuses on a separate step in the process; subsequent chapters build on the work you did in the previous ones. At the end of this book are worksheets and important documents that will assist you in personalizing your search, including the health/safety and background-check requirements necessary for your desired candidate. These same worksheets and important documents can also be downloaded at the Institute for Families and Nannies website: https://www.tiffan.org.

Beyond checklists and process, *The Nanny Manual* is about the relationship parents create with their nanny. It is about using your heart, your soul and your mind. Hiring the right nanny is no easy task, primarily because it is such an important decision and fraught with expectations. All parents want the best for their child. What is more important than ensuring the person who spends a good part of most days of the week during your child's very early years is giving the best care possible? If you approach this process with your heart, mind and soul, choosing the person you want to create a relationship with in order to help you care for your child can be one of the most challenging, yet rewarding decisions of your life.

MELISSA'S STORY

"Mom—let's invite all the nannies who took care of us since we were babies over to the house for dinner next week!"

Nothing in Melissa's 17 years of motherhood had ever prepared her for this request! "Why would we want to do this?" was her first thought. But Melissa paused. She knew that while her kids were pretty good at answering open-ended questions on an exam, any question from her that started with the word why received the simple and frustrating answer, "Just because." Instead, Melissa said, "Sure, why not? It will be great to see everyone again! You make the arrangements. I'm all for it!"

Truth be told, nannies and childcare seemed like ancient history to Melissa. Jacob and Sarah were now well into their teen years and those earlier years of teaming up with a nanny to change diapers, make bottles, settle temper tantrums and teach the kids how to get along with each other had morphed into getting to and from competitive soccer games, preparing for college entrance exams and the drama of teen relationships.

Melissa had worked full-time since her eldest, Jacob, was three months old. The first nanny she hired was Maria. Maria was recommended by a colleague at work and was known to be very nurturing, loving, honest and great with babies. Melissa's second child, Sarah, was born two years later, and Maria stayed on to take care of both kids. She would get the kids dressed, fed and ready for the day, walk Jacob to preschool and take care of Sarah until the preschool pickup. After that it was off to the park, then home and dinner. Melissa would get home around 6 p.m. and take over the night routines from there.

Soon, Sarah started kindergarten and Melissa had a difficult decision to make. The kids needed someone to drive them back and forth to school and help with homework. Maria didn't drive, and the rudimentary education she had back in El Salvador wasn't sufficient to help Jacob with his homework. Melissa went through the agonizing process of letting Maria go. She hired her second nanny, Katie, a graduate student. Katie was vastly different from Maria and according to Jacob and Sarah, "just awesome!" She was young, tall, athletic, dark-skinned and rode a motorcycle. The kids were incredibly proud when she picked them up from school, and invitations to their friends for play dates were never turned down! Katie stayed on full-time for the next four years, followed by two graduate students who became, like Katie, big sisters and role models for Jacob and Sarah.

During the "nanny dinner," Melissa watched and listened as everyone shared their stories of what they had done together. They remembered the places they went, what they did, the people who had been part of their lives back then. They laughed at all the things that went right and those that were near-disasters! The day they were locked out of the house; the day the puppy arrived; the day Sarah cried when her best friend didn't want to hang out with her; the day Jacob had a meltdown at the fancy restaurant because they didn't have pizza. And, yes, the photo album Maria gave them when she left had been taken out of Sarah's closet and every photo became another story.

Later that night after everyone had said their good-byes, Melissa realized that she had done what was right for herself as a working mother, and for her kids. Everything had gone okay. Her kids would be fine.

But Melissa clearly remembers the conflicts she felt over the years when she didn't know what to expect or how to feel. These conflicts emanated from gut-wrenching, emotionally charged questions. Am I doing right by myself as a mom and by my kids? Am I causing harm?

What will be the outcome? Can I trust that my nanny is doing right by my kids and me? There was always a risk and absolutely no guarantees.

Looking back, Melissa remembered how incredibly rough it was as a first-time mom with a newborn, going through the process of hiring a nanny for the first time. It was not an easy task.

Jacob was just six weeks old, and Melissa was tired and cranky from sleep deprivation. Her emotions were so unpredictable she hardly knew who she was most days. One moment she felt maternal, female and settled, full of milk and love and satiated with joy. In an instant, this budding maternal confidence eroded and she was awash with feelings of incompetence. The realization that this baby—her baby— was completely dependent on her for survival swept over Melissa. Jacob cried for food and only she could produce it. He cried when his diaper was wet and it was she who knew why he was crying. He cried for no apparent reason, and she had to figure out what he wanted and fix it. She had to do something, anything to make whatever was not right okay again. It was incessant, 24 hours a day, every day, without a break.

Melissa had hit the wall. She called her best friend, Stephanie, who had some advice. "You need someone who will come at night and take care of Jacob so you can get a good night's sleep. Most moms hire this kind of help now. Call Maria. She's been doing this for years. You'll love her. She's so maternal!" Stephanie's advice sounded so right and so wise. Just the idea that a good night's sleep was a phone call away was comforting! Melissa called Maria, who sounded just as Stephanie described her—maternal and warm. In her worn-out state, Melissa asked a few questions that made little sense, and they agreed Maria would come at 10 o'clock that night.

When Melissa opened the door, there stood this sweet woman, hair pulled back from her light brown face, with kind eyes and a soft, rounded body. Her voice was soothing and confident. After a brief exchange, Maria simply said to Melissa, "You're tired; go to bed. Let me have the baby."

That's when the panic set in. Give you my baby? You want me to give you my baby? You expect me to go into another room, go to sleep and leave him with you? Melissa wondered, What was I thinking? How can I leave my baby who is so dependent on me? How can I leave him with someone who is a complete stranger and make sure he is safe and cared for? How can I trust someone I've known for such a short time with this huge responsibility? How will I know that she'll know what he needs? Will Jacob feel abandoned by the very person he depends on for survival?

What kind of mother am I, anyway?

Slowly, over the next few weeks together, Melissa learned to trust Maria. The maternal warmth Maria exuded was comforting to Melissa and she could see that Jacob was comforted also. That need to feel comforted herself, the same way she wanted Jacob to feel, came as a surprise to Melissa. They were both getting what they needed from Maria.

Several months later, this blissful ambiance was punctured. It happened at the end of an exhausting day at work. Melissa looked forward to coming home, where she could shed her work clothes, her work life, its responsibilities, the stress and "be mom." It would be so comforting to cuddle with Jacob! They would look at his favorite books together, reading the same ones over and over, but making it a little different each time. They would laugh at the antics of the bear, or discover yet again where the rabbit was hiding. It would be their world, just the two of them, doing what they loved to do together.

When Melissa walked in the door, there was Maria reading to Jacob. They were laughing and reading Jacob's favorite book. The imagined magic had lost its allure, but it wasn't until Maria exclaimed excitedly that Jacob took his first step that day that Melissa lost it. In Melissa's mind, Maria not only had taken away the special time with her son that she longed for, but had robbed her of a moment in Jacob's life that she could never get again—Jacob's first step.

Melissa sought comfort with Stephanie. Just dumping out her rage, fear, jealousy, sense of inadequacy and confusion helped. Stephanie knew the words of reason to soften the sharp edges. Still, Melissa learned there are experiences mothers have that can't be fixed, understood or massaged into reasonableness. These moments hurt.

The sting abated over time. After all, there were plenty of moments in Melissa's life with Jacob that shored up her identity as a mom. Stephanie and other women at work contributed to that feeling. Rides in the backseat of a taxi, heading to an off-site meeting, became stolen moments to bare their souls about their kids and the challenges of raising them while working. One of these encounters brought tears and some insight. Melissa was sharing her concerns about working while also raising Jacob. She wasn't sure she was doing the right thing by working and wouldn't know until years later. If things did go wrong, she wouldn't be able to undo it. Laughingly Melissa said, "He'll be in therapy for life because of my decision!" Her friend became quiet and asked, "Did your mom work when you were three months old?" Melissa's mom had been at home until Melissa started kindergarten and she wasn't ecstatic about Melissa working. There were some strained discussions about this when Jacob was born. Raised to be a successful career woman, Melissa had adopted Facebook COO Sheryl Sandberg's battle cry of "leaning in" to her career long before Sandberg issued these marching orders to thousands of young women rising into the ranks.[1] How could Melissa now turn her back on the many years she'd been working to succeed? Her colleague's

---

1   Sheryl Sandberg, Commencement Speech, Barnard College, May 18, 2011.

question gave her pause, and she reflected on what had been missed with her march forward to do it all.

In spite of all the forward strides and policy changes achieved to support working mothers, no one told them how to accomplish the balancing act or how they might feel about doing it. Melissa and the large cohort of women of her generation were forging new territory. Melissa's concerns about the outcome were expectable. Yet they were more worrisome because Melissa couldn't imagine what it would have been like to have been raised by a mom who worked when she was three months old. As Melissa's colleague noted, "How can you imagine what Jacob's experience could be if you haven't experienced it yourself?"

Maternal emotions don't run a steady course or settle down just because you figured out why you're feeling a certain way. One Saturday morning, Melissa went to get Jacob's cereal down from the top shelf. She sang out, "Here are the Cheerios for breakfast!" Jacob, using his newly found big-boy voice of independence, declared, "No, Mommy—that's not what I have for breakfast. I eat Rice Krispies." Melissa was defeated and deflated. What kind of mother doesn't know her son's favorite breakfast cereal? Visions of Maria lovingly handing a bowl of Rice Krispies to Jacob each morning—a ritual they shared between them and no one else—sent chills through Melissa's spine. She was jealous. She felt excluded and incompetent. At that moment, she hated Maria and she hated herself.

To understand Melissa's strong response and conflicted feelings about being in control, it helps to know more about her background. Melissa grew up in Berkeley, a bedrock of liberalism. She drank the Kool-Aid of feminism from the earliest of ages, fueled by the lyrics of the Gloria Gaynor's song "I Will Survive." When Sarah was born, Melissa felt an unexpected sense of sisterhood emerge between them. Unlike with Jacob, Sarah's toddler defiance meant strength, autonomy, independence! Sarah would stand on her own, shout to the world who she is and make her own decisions without the conscriptions of the establishment defining gender roles. When tripping over memories of the evening of the Nanny dinner, Melissa flashed back to the gift Maria gave Sarah for her fourth birthday. It was—shockingly—a Barbie doll, complete with the frilliest dress and highest heels ever! Melissa wanted to snatch that icon—the "quintessential blond bimbo"[2]—away from Sarah's adoring eyes. What was Maria teaching Sarah anyway during those hours they spent together day in and day out? Would the mother-daughter sisterhood Melissa was forging be shattered? In her teen years, would Sarah defiantly claim the principles of dependency and a woman's right to be "barefoot, pregnant and in the kitchen"? Would she be singing "Stand by Your Man" instead of "I Will Survive"?

Melissa could laugh at the situation now. Barbie hadn't destroyed Sarah's independence. Sarah was a self-confident young woman, and seemingly less defiant, more secure, more open-minded and more accepting of differences than Melissa had been at her age. Melissa attributed this to having relationships with women that chose different life paths and held different value systems, including Maria. If it "takes a village to raise a child," then in Melissa's eyes, this village can include people with a variety of differences and the child won't be "broken."

Melissa remembered being asked by Jacob on the way to school one morning why she still worked when a lot of his friends' moms didn't. When she told him she had a really good job and loved what she was doing, Jacob said: "Wow, that's cool!"

---

2   Miriam Forman-Brunnell, "What Barbie Dolls Have to Say about Post-War American Culture," University of Missouri, Kansas City, Missouri. http://www.smithsonianeducation.org/idealabs/ap/essays/barbie.htm

FROM THE VILLAGE TO THE BOARDROOM

. . . .

With the rapid rise in the number of American mothers in the workforce comes a concurrent change in the culture of caregiving in the U.S. Once considered to be the responsibility of the nuclear family with the mother as the provider of care, the work of mothering is now outsourced to another—a nanny, preschool teacher, grandparent or family daycare provider—for what can be long hours of the day. Alongside this reality is a profound ambivalence in American culture about who is responsible for and who is raising the kids. This ambivalence is seen in the U.S. Government's policies to move mothers into the workforce after six weeks or three months of maternity leave while providing little financial or childcare support for a mother to manage work and family. We witness ambivalence in the polarization of arguments on whether American women should "opt in" or "opt out" of their careers while raising a family. We again witness ambivalence in the persistence of the Myth of the Perfect Mother, personified by June Cleaver, alongside the modern myth of the Working Mother who can "do it all" perfectly well. If we are ambivalent about the inclusion of a nanny, the "third" into the family constellation, then how are we to begin to think about what arrangement would be good enough or optimal for our families?

The "New" Mother: It Takes a Village

The phrase "it takes a village" became popular after Hillary Clinton published her book of the same name in 1996.[3] Borrowed from the traditional African proverb "It takes a village to raise a child," the book underscores not only the necessity but the importance of children being raised not only by parents, but also by other caring adults who are thoroughly invested in the child's well-being. This may include grandparents, aunts, uncles, teachers, neighbors, and especially the people we'll be talking about in this book—nannies.

For most of history, villages were responsible for childcare, with women concentrating on homemaking and child-rearing together while the men went off to work on the farm or at the family business. Families were generally located in the same geographical area, with entire generations living in the same town. Grandparents, aunts or older cousins stepped in to help mothers with young children.

Hiring someone to care for one's child is not new in this country. In the 18th and 19th centuries, affluent families hired nannies–the idealized version we've come to know through the character of Mary Poppins. At the beginning of the 20th century, 18% of American women were in the workforce. With the rise of the Feminist Movement in the 1970s, that number rose to 38%. By 2014 the percentage of women in the workforce was over 57%.[4] More poignantly, in 2015 the percentage of American children living in married-couple households where both parents worked was 61%[5]. Now, in the 21st century, it is commonplace for women to be both in the workplace and full-time mothers.

---

3   Hillary Rodham Clinton, *It Takes a Village* (New York: Simon & Schuster, 1996).

4   "Labor and Employment," *Women in the Labor Force*, Infoplease. http://www.infoplease. com/ipa/A0104673.html

5   *Employment Characteristics of Families—2015*, Bureau of Labor Statistics, U.S. Department of Labor, April 22, 2016, p. 2. https://www.bls.gov/news.release/pdf/famee.pdf

The village was different among the royalty or affluent families of the 19th and 20th centuries. These families used outside help, a position usually known as a "nurse," who was in charge of the nursery along with assistants known as nursemaids. These women, later termed nannies, were servants and spent their lives in the home of their masters, often from childhood until old age. Because of their deep involvement in raising the children of the family, nannies were often remembered with great affection and treated more kindly than the junior servants. Some nannies remained in the employment of the same aristocratic family for years, looking after successive generations of children.[6] Unlike the servant nanny of yesterday, this type of caregiving has been redefined as the role of a governess and has become embodied in the caricatures of the magical English nanny, Mary Poppins, and Maria von Trapp, her Austrian counterpart from *The Sound of Music*.

Whether the village was made up of relatives, neighbors or nannies, helping mothers raise healthy children was part of the social and cultural value system. Caregiving was an expectation dictated by cultural norms for the common good. In American and European working-class families, older siblings cared for their younger siblings, and aunties and grandparents took charge of little ones when needed. In the developing nations of Indonesia, India and Tibet, in the small towns of the Philippines, Pacific Islands and Latin America, the village extended beyond just family to the whole community. A village child was everyone's child. In these villages, caregiving was not a job. It was what one did as part of the fabric of the community. It was a seamless expectation, part of the social contract, and it was reinforced by the unstated assumption that this is simply what one does to be a member of the community.

---

6   Nanny. https://en.wikipedia.org/wiki/Nanny

The beginning of the 21st century ushered in a new era of mothers working outside the home. In 1948, only 17% of married mothers were in the labor force. By the 1980s, labor force participation had become an integral part of their lives. In 1985, 61% of married mothers were working or looking for work. By 1995, their labor force participation rate had reached 70%. In 2005, the participation rate of married mothers with preschoolers was 60%. The percentage of married mothers with children under a year old in 2000 was 53.3%. The participation rate of married mothers of school-age children was 75% in 2005.[7] This data does not include participation rates of single-parent households, which would increase these rates to even more significant levels.

But for the 21st-century American working mother, the culture of caregiving is changing. The majority of mothers with children under five years old are in the workforce and extended family is not nearby for childcare support. As a result, getting outside help—such as a nanny—to care for children has become more of a necessity than a luxury. Hiring a nanny has moved down the socioeconomic ladder from a caregiving practice used solely by the affluent to one now used by the middle and working classes. Paying for childcare has also changed cultural norms and the way we view the relationship between mothers and nannies. Along with these changes comes an ongoing and profound ambivalence in American culture about how we care for children, how we view working mothers, and how we regard nannies and the caregiving roles they perform.

Two very high-profile speeches have sparked heated debates among women about whether mothers should "lean in" to their careers or "opt out" of the workplace until their children leave home. Facebook COO Sheryl Sandberg's commencement address at Barnard College in 2011,

---

[7]   *"Trends in Labor Force Participation of Married Mothers of Infants,"* Married Mothers in the Labor Force, Monthly Labor Review, February 2007, p. 9.

as well as her subsequent TED Talk, advised women, "Do not leave before you leave. Do not lean back; lean in. Put your foot on that gas pedal and keep it there until the day you have to make a decision, and then make a decision. That's the only way, when that day comes, you'll even have a decision to make."[8] On the other side of the spectrum, Princeton University professor Anne-Marie Slaughter made waves the following year with an article in *The Atlantic*, "Why Women Still Can't Have It All,"[9] which underscores why a professional high-level career does not mix with caring for children in our society. Central to the debate are questions modern moms face. Who is raising the kids? What price do we pay by choosing to lean in or opt out?

Having a Viable Choice

To lean in or opt out, that is the question. But should it really be a question at all? The bifurcation of the issue implies that a mother has a viable choice. Yet as mothers who choose to lean in to their career recognize very quickly, this choice becomes viable only when they can afford to pay for quality childcare. It also means having access to quality childcare so that they can work. For mothers who choose to opt out, it means that they, their families and communities truly recognize that there is inherent value in mothering. Unless affordable, high-quality childcare arrangements are available and there is recognition that there is high value in the work of mothering, going back to work or opting out of the workforce are not even viable or easy choices for mothers.

---

8   Sheryl Sandberg, "Why We Have Few Women Leaders," Ted Talk, December 2010. https://www.ted.com/speakers/sheryl_sandberg

9   Anne-Marie Slaughter, "Why Women Still Can't Have It All," *The Atlantic*, July/August 2012. http://www.theatlantic.com/magazine/archive/2012/07/why-women-still-cant-have-it-all/309020/

A Working Mother's Challenge

The challenge for working mothers in the 21st century goes beyond the "lean in" argument. How can a working mother reconcile her dual responsibilities to work and mothering without feeling she is failing in both? Working mothers today benefit from changes in workplace support accomplished by 20th-century feminists, such as job sharing, flexible work schedules, family medical leave and childcare resource and referral services. Yet what the Feminist Movement failed to acknowledge, and what is often left out of public discourse, are the conflicting and unexpectedly strong emotions a working mother experiences over leaving her child with a caregiver, a person who is most often a complete stranger to her. Profound questions inevitably must be understood and reconciled before working mothers can return to the workforce and be competent in their work. These questions include: Am I abdicating my responsibility as a mother to my child? Am I causing harm? Can I trust this nanny? If I do work, what will the outcome be for my child, my family and me?

Over the past 20 years, a substantial body of research shows that children have the capacity to create unique, loving relationships with those adults responsible for caring for them. Research also shows that children can discriminate between individuals showing certain preferences within these relationships. We know from research and practical experience that children know who Mom and Dad are. In the nanny-parent relationship, however, the green-eyed monster isn't always rational. The desire to be "Mom," to have exclusivity over your child's love, to feel competent and in control is a powerful emotion that can rock even the most secure, self-confident woman.

The Stay-at-Home Mother

The decision to opt out of the workforce doesn't come easily. For some women, it's a matter of economics. Can they afford to work and pay for childcare? For some women, it's a matter of dissatisfaction with the available childcare options. For some, the idea of handing over childcare responsibility to a stranger is such an anathema to their identity as a mother that almost by default they choose to stay home. For others, caring for children is what they want to do because of the intrinsic satisfaction it brings to them.

Regardless of the basis for the decision, many stay-at-home modern moms need help to manage the daily household responsibilities and care of children. Hiring a nanny or "mother's helper" is the solution.

One might expect issues of trust or outcome would be minimized in mothers who are at home with their nanny. A working mother's worry about how her child is being cared for would be ameliorated if she were around to observe and manage the care. While this makes for commonsense reasoning, mothers at home can neither micromanage care successfully nor completely control outcomes. Quality childcare workers must be caring and attentive. Allowing another to care for children in a responsible manner requires an element of trust that the person doing the work will perform it in a way that is intentional and according to your desired outcome. Whether a mother is at home or at work, allowing a nanny to do the work of a mother involves accepting a level of uncertainty about outcome and of letting go of the need to control everything.

Mothers at home working alongside their nanny navigate this emotional land mine constantly, and most stay-at-home moms would argue their hearts can often overrule reason. If a nanny does her work well, then children thrive. Who then is responsible for the outcome—mom or nanny? Mothers observe first-hand situations when their nanny is able to soothe their crying baby easily, consistently set limits and get picky eaters to eat vegetables. Envy, jealousy and feelings of inadequacy visit all mothers who hire nannies, whether the choice is to be a stay-at-home mom or a working mother.

The Inner Life of the Mother

This decision to hire a nanny can wreak havoc on a woman's psyche. When a mother makes this decision, she is faced with the reality and responsibility of creating a relationship with her nanny that fits with herself as a new mother.

Daniel Stern, in his definitive 1995 book, *The Motherhood Constellation,*[10] and 1998 work, *The Birth of a Mother,*[11] describes the process and challenges a new mother goes through to integrate her other known identities as a woman, wife or partner with her new role as a mother. Dr. Stern proposes that new mothers create a "motherhood constellation," or a self-identity that is organized around the presence and care of her infant. Within this constellation of mutual recognition, a mother is poignantly aware of her new responsibility for the life of another human being; of her capacity to meet the complete dependency needs of her baby and her need for support—a maternal matrix—in order to do so. A mother draws from her own experience of having been mothered as a beginning template upon which to form her self-identity.

But what if this 21st-century mother was raised by a mother who did not return to the workforce, but instead stayed home caring for her children?

---

10   Daniel N. Stern, M.D., *The Motherhood Constellation* (London: Karnac Books, Ltd.), 112.
11   Daniel N. Stern, M.D., *The Birth of a Mother: How the Motherhood Experience Changes You Forever* (New York: Basic Books, 1998).

While today's millennial parents are more likely to have been raised in families where both parents worked, during the first fifteen years of my practice, I found that the vast majority of first-time mothers in the San Francisco Bay Area were raised by a stay-at-home mother who did not use hired help. A woman can find it very difficult to imagine how to mother differently than her mother did and to know what the outcome would be if she tried. The resultant guilt and ambivalence that mothers feel about leaving their children in the care of another often dictates how well they put together a quality childcare arrangement that works. Those feelings can influence when they choose to begin the process of hiring a nanny and can also affect the nanny they choose. For example, a highly anxious working mother may characteristically "take control" and start her nanny search during her third trimester of pregnancy. The decision becomes part of her checklist of to-do items, along with putting together the nursery or creating a birth plan. She may find, however, that the nanny she chooses before the baby is born doesn't fit well after she holds her baby in her arms for the first time Another anxious mother may enter a state of denial about hiring a nanny, convincing herself that there is plenty of time to sort things out during maternity leave and then, in a panic two weeks before that leave ends, realize time has run out. She then faces the untenable pressure of having to begin an arduous and time-consuming process to make this most important decision about her baby's care in a short amount of time.

Regardless of the challenges a woman faces around her identity as a mother, these feelings of guilt and ambivalence are intensified because of the baby's complete dependency on her for survival. What may have been a pragmatic decision before the baby was born often becomes highly emotional after. As Daphne de Marneffe describes so poignantly in her book *Maternal Desire*, there exists an often unspoken yet strong desire and a resultant satisfaction that a mother experiences in nurturing and caring for her baby.[12] This strong urge to protect and nurture her newborn conflicts with her decision to return to work and hire a nanny to take on part of the maternal role of caring for her baby.

It's not only possible to find a nanny you can trust, it's essential that you do so for your own well-being and the good of your children. While it's reasonable to have high expectations, it's also important that you take a realistic approach. Through books, television, movies and more, we've all been influenced by the myth of the perfect nanny. Before you can come to grips with what you need, want and can reasonably expect in a nanny, let's take a close look at one of our beloved icons, Mary Poppins.

Mary Poppins: Why This Pervasive Myth Endures

In the 1964 film version of *Mary Poppins*, Jane and Michael Banks's wishes for a nanny included a cheery disposition, rosy cheeks and no warts. Miraculously, this idealized nanny appeared out of the blue, required no training, worked whenever needed, knew her place and never asked for a paycheck. Nowadays, equally optimistic parents want their own version of Mary Poppins: someone who will show up on their doorstep when they need her, someone who is responsible and reliable, who will stay for as long as necessary and who will not take over their role as parent or put a dent in their family finances. As a cultural icon, Mary Poppins represents a family's wish for a nanny who is easy to find, loving, honest, fun, familiar and affordable—someone who "fits in" with their family.

---

12 Daphne de Marneffe, *Maternal Desire* (New York: Little Brown and Company, 2004), 152–53.

Who Is Mary Poppins?

She is a mystery.

When you picture Mary Poppins, what do you see? Many people imagine Julie Andrews and her musical way with children, but the character is older than that and more complex. Created by the Australian-born novelist P. L. Travers, the first Mary Poppins book was published in 1934, and the last of the eight-part series in 1988. Travers's magical nanny has entranced generations of parents and children, but just who is the enigmatic figure of Mary Poppins and why does she remain the mythical ideal?

As with all mysteries, the character of Mary Poppins is one to be pondered again and again. Mary Travers created her to be amorphous, full of ambiguity and intrigue—a unique and enchanting character for young children and a complex one for adults to hang their hopes and dreams upon.

She is strangely familiar.

Mary Poppins arrived without a personal history, title or the expectation that the Banks family would want to know anything about her. We know the story is a work of fiction, but the fact that Travers chose to create her character without a history is still remarkable given her central role in the Banks family, the great responsibility she was given to educate and care for the children and the designated place she held in society. She is on one level a total stranger who flies in on the wind and at another level someone the Banks family trusted almost implicitly with their children. Mary Poppins was never "anything more than 'strangely familiar.'"

She is competent.

Although she hardly came across as a modern-day "baby whisperer," Mary Poppins seemed to know almost intuitively about children and their development. She didn't rely on words to communicate her knowledge but operated intelligently in the world of the nonverbal. She could bring order to the Banks household, manage the aggression and manipulations of the children, pique their curiosities and indulge their fantasies—all while also molding them to fit into the social structure of their day. Oh, and she could sing.

What Does Mary Poppins Represent?

The mystery of who Mary Poppins really was sheds light on the social and cultural changes facing Western society in how we care for young children. As mothers continue to seek nonfamilial childcare support, we also search for answers to who nannies are and the roles they play. Nannies do the work of mothering and yet they are not the mothers. Nannies have become "strangely familiar" to us, blurring the boundaries between what they do and what moms do. While we may not want to acknowledge our nanny as doing the work of mothering, we also want her and need her. Our ambivalence and reluctance is most evident in the fact that as a society, we have yet to universally acknowledge nannies as childcare professionals among the ranks of infant/toddler and preschool teachers. Nannies remain an unlicensed and unregulated cohort of individuals performing a vastly important role in children's lives.

This ambivalence often translates into making nannies invisible members of the family and of society, as Susan Scheftel, PhD, so poignantly describes in her paper "Why Aren't We Curious about Nannies?"[13]

---

13   Susan Scheftel, "Why Aren't We Curious about Nannies?", in *The Psychoanalytic Study of the Child 66* (New Haven, CT: Yale University Press, 2012).

We want all of what Mary Poppins offers and yet we are very ambivalent about having her at all. Confronting and dealing with this ambivalence is the first step in the process of deciding what you need in a nanny and finding that "right fit" for your family.

2 WHEN WISHFUL THINKING MEETS REALITY

···

The Elusive Search for Mary Poppins

It should come as no surprise that many parents feel conflicted as they decide whether to continue to work or stay home after their child is born. Shouldn't a mother be home to nurture and raise her child just as her mother did? Isn't that her role as a parent? If mothers decide to return to work and hire a nanny, are they abdicating their role and sending the wrong message to the next generation? The myth of Mary Poppins perpetuates the idea that the perfect nanny is not only available but exists in the first place. These outsized expectations crash into reality when parents start the process of looking for a nanny, and can crop up repeatedly as the ongoing relationship with a nanny is forged. Having realistic expectations going into the process can save parents a world of time and heartache.

Following is a list of the things parents wish for—and the reality they discover.

An easy, simple and quick search

Post a few ads online, receive a few applications, and voilà! The perfect nanny is found. This scenario, though unlikely, is what many parents imagine and wish for when they think of hiring a nanny. The harsh reality can be quite the opposite. The challenge for parents, whether doing a self-search or using the services of a nanny placement agency, is how to choose a stranger who has all the ideal traits of Mary Poppins while recognizing that the market comprises a vast assortment of women, many of whom have these skills and many more who don't.

A known entity: Someone we can trust

In the U.S., literally anyone can post a notice online, on a church bulletin board or through word of mouth that they want to care for children. Compare that to someone working in a childcare center who must present proper credentials in order to get the job. A working mother begins her nanny search in this frightening arena, entering a market of unlicensed and unregulated caregivers, many of whom should never be caring for children in the first place. The most worrisome issue a mother confronts as she begins the search process for a nanny is finding someone she can trust.

Wisdom and knowledge: Someone who knows intuitively how to care for kids

Mr. and Mrs. Banks didn't have to tell Mary Poppins what to do. In fact, they were barely involved at all, and yet this magical nanny took perfect charge of everything from loving and caring for each of the children to cleaning their rooms and overseeing their bedtime routine. Mary Poppins never left a messy kitchen, dirty children, clothes unwashed or a reheated takeout meal on the table. She didn't require a checklist or daily reminder about the children's schedule or prioritization of responsibilities. This type of nanny is every mom's dream. In the 21st century, the expectation that chaos turns into order effortlessly has become a magical notion that colors the world of childcare.

This nanny is an apparition, but a real person as well. She has a mission to keep the children safe and the home fires burning. Mary Poppins makes the children feel secure because she can contain their aggression and balance their frustration and gratification while remaining unflappable and powerful.

Boundaries: She knows her place

Mary Poppins knew when to take charge of a situation as well as when to step away and let the family have private bonding time. At the end of the Disney film, Mary's magical umbrella speaks to her, saying, "You know, they think more of their father than they do of you." Mary replies, "That's as it should be."[14] Parents want to ensure their role is primary, both as an employer to their nanny and as parents to their children.

While the modernized concept of "boundaries" wasn't part of the early-20th-century vernacular, Mary Poppins never overstepped them. She seemed to have the understanding that it is a mother's role to provide safe, responsible, nurturing and loving care for her child. Giving that responsibility to someone who is a virtual stranger is not easily done, and when a mom does hand it over, she does so with the unspoken expectation that her nanny doesn't step into her territory and usurp her role as mom. A good nanny understands the mother's concerns and acts accordingly.

---

14   *Mary Poppins*, starring Julie Andrews and Dick Van Dyke. Directed by Robert Stevenson; produced by Walt Disney, 1964.

Affordability: She works for love, not money

Mary Poppins worked 24 hours a day, every day, for as long as the Banks family needed her. She didn't receive a paycheck or benefits. It was assumed she worked for love—not for money.

Paying someone to love your children can seem counterintuitive, but that's exactly what parents do when they hire a nanny. The feminist economist Nancy Folbre, who focuses on economics and the family, questions this odd exchange in her book *The Invisible Heart: Economics and Family Values*. As an employer, how can a parent know what she is paying for? A nanny is paid to be attentive, loving and caring. Is it possible to itemize and quantify the kind and amount of caring acts she provides? Do the cold, harsh rules of commerce apply? Should we expect nannies to leave and stop loving a child if a better offer comes their way, if the responsibilities are too great or if the demands of the child seem impossible to manage?[15] When you pay a nanny to care for your child, you are faced with challenging your most basic assumptions, made explicit by the Beatles' song "Money Can't Buy Me Love."

Consider the family budget. Apart from sticker shock at the $20-to-$30-per-hour market rates prevalent in some urban areas for nannies in 2017, and with few government- or employer-sponsored childcare subsidies, the idea of paying someone to "mother" one's child seems an oxymoron. Sociologist Arlie Hochschild, in her social-feminist writings on the modern family, notes that paying a stranger to care for a child moves the work of mothering from the world of home into the world of commerce and commodities. Dr. Hochschild poses the question: Is it possible to pay someone to be warm, nurturing and loving? Can you purchase caring?[16]

---

15   Nancy Folbre, *The Invisible Heart: Economics and Family Values* (New York: The New Press, 2001).

16   Arlie Hochschild, *The Commercialization of Intimate Life* (Berkeley: University of California Press, 2003).

A nanny is the modern-day version of Mary Poppins. She is someone who fits in seamlessly with a family to make the difficult work of parenting easier. Are today's parents prepared for this new paradigm in parenting? In both emotional and practical terms, the data suggests they may not be. Also, unlike parenting in the 1960s, today the vast majority of mothers work and the role of fathers is no longer relegated primarily to "bringing home the bacon," but requires them to take a greater role in the care of the children. Many choose to be a stay-at-home dad and take on the daily responsibilities for raising their children.[17]

The Right Fit versus the Perfect Fit: Six Basic Assumptions

The Nanny Manual is based on several key assumptions about parents and nannies, garnered from my direct experience as well as from societal trends and research. Understanding these assumptions will help you determine what you really need in a caregiver: someone who is right for you and your children, rather than that elusive "perfect" nanny.

This book starts with the basic assumption that all parents need help caring for their children at different times in their children's lives. Some parents have family and friends—people they know and trust—to lend a helping hand. Others do not. Among those without family or friends available, many hire nannies.

There has been a significant diversification in the kinds of childcare arrangements parents create in order to match the needs of their families. The cost of childcare, coupled with the lack of openings in quality childcare centers or family childcare homes for infants and toddlers, has created a new demand for share-care arrangements.

---

17   http://www.pewsocialtrends.org/2014/06/05/growing-number-of-dads-home-with-the-kids/

Parents are now partnering with other parents to hire a nanny who provides care for the children of both in either one or both families' homes, thus sharing the cost of care and increasing parenting support. Some families decide to job-share the care of the children. One parent will care for the children of the other part of the time, swapping days with the other family and hiring a nanny for backup care or additional care on evenings and weekends. Some families who have achieved a considerable measure of economic success add one, two or even more nannies to their household staff to manage their hectic personal, family and work lives.

The second assumption is that the type of childcare assistance parents need can be quite different among families and it can change over time. Some parents decide a mother's helper or family assistant is best for them at a particular time in their family life instead of a full-charge nanny. Others need only a babysitter to lend a hand for a few hours a couple of days each week. Many families start with a nanny when their child is an infant and then need a different form of care during the preschool years.

The third assumption is that all parents want the best care for their children and that every nanny wants to work for parents who respect what she does and the care she gives. In this way, parents and nannies create a partnership to care for the children.

The fourth assumption is that there are different parents, different families, different children and different nannies. While a particular nanny might work beautifully for one family, she could be a poor match for another. It is all about the right fit.

The fifth assumption is that finding a nanny is not always an easy task. The market for nannies is unlicensed and unregulated. There are few government resources to assist parents in finding and keeping honest, trustworthy and competent nannies. In this way, the burden falls on parents to separate the legitimate, loving nanny from the rest.

The sixth assumption is that finding and choosing a nanny is both a pragmatic and an emotional process. How you feel about asking a complete stranger to care for your child can influence when you start looking, how you conduct the search and which nanny you choose. There are expectable worries and common misperceptions that can prevent parents from choosing the right nanny.

BRIGIT'S STORY

I Can't Make a Decision

Brigit was a perfectionist. Everything she did had to be perfect and done perfectly well. So, she started her nanny search in her 3rd trimester. The baby would be born in July, there would be a full-time nanny with infant experience hired and Brigit would go back to working part time in August ramping up to full time in September. Check.

She interviewed five nannies. Each had over six years' experience caring for infants and toddlers, had worked at least three years with one family, had either early childhood education or self-taught knowledge of child development and excellent references for character and honesty.

Everyone waited for the decision. Brigit couldn't make it. No one seemed right. Back to the drawing boards. Character and honesty moved up and knowledge of child development went into the 'preferred category'. All Brigit's friends advised her: if your nanny loves your child, that's enough.

For Brigit, something was missing from this decision. Feelings. Brigit couldn't feel a connection with any of the candidates in a way that said, this is right. They all seemed loving and warm in various degrees but Brigit couldn't feel that "aha" moment she wanted.

This nagged Brigit. She wanted this gut feeling, an "aha" moment telling her that the person was right. One day while shedding her physician 'white coat' persona for quieter moments at home, she realized what was missing from the interviews – the baby. Without seeing the nanny holding and caring for her baby, a very important contribution to having an "aha" moment wasn't there. The interviews had a familiar, somewhat 'corporate' tone to them.

But Brigit couldn't wait for the baby to be born. A decision had to be made and it had to be right and it had to be now before the baby was in hers or a nanny candidate's arms.

So, Brigit interviewed 3 more candidates. She hired Anne. Check.

Joy, the most beautiful child ever, was born a week later.

Anne started when Joy was 8 days old. A week later, Brigit let her go. There was a long list of pro's and con's. They all pointed to a lack of trust. First of all, Anne didn't seem at ease with Joy. She jiggled her too much; she talked annoyingly all the time and in a high-pitch tone that irritated Brigit. And then there was the inconsistency in following instructions. Everything had its right place in Joy's room. The baby wipes should always be in this part of the changing table. The dirty baby bottles had to be put in the bottle washer immediately after use. Why were the baby wipes on the dresser at the end of the day?   Why were the dirty bottles left in the sink? Brigit went over the expectations list with Anne every morning but always there was something not correct. Even though Anne seemed loving and sweet to Joy, wasn't it obvious the lack of follow-through with bottles and wipes would slip into the realm of Joy's care?

Brigit knew she made the right decision to fire Anne but now she was anxious. Could she trust her judgment? Would anyone be right?

It was a tough next round of interviews. Brigit waivered. How could she be a perfect mother and make another disastrous decision? How could she be so indecisive??

She needed childcare. Simple. She hired based on character. Gloria was warm, loving, non-intrusive, experienced. She was also deferential and wanted to please. Joy was definitely in loving hands. Gloria adored her. This was obvious. But Gloria's need to please grated and unnerved Brigit. She would ask, "Do you want Joy to go out for her walk now?" or "Should I wake her now for a feeding?" Brigit went into this hire feeling indecisive. She wanted her nanny to make decisions and relieve her from having to make decisions she had very limited knowledge about. Brigit told Gloria to use her best judgment. But Gloria's wish to please overrode use of judgment. Indecisiveness hovered around both Brigit and Gloria. Not a perfect hire.

Joy was now 2 months old. She had two nannies, both failures. She would get a third.

At this point in time, Brigit was back at work. She was compelled to fulfill her commitment as a physician that could balance work and family. She wanted to be a role model for other female doctors rising in the ranks. But the nanny problem strained her. The stress of not having the right and perfect fit nanny wore her down. Brigit got a recommendation from a relative. How could she argue with positive reviews from family? She hired Paula.

Paula was nurturing and caring but Brigit wasn't 100% sure. She felt Paula provided quiet, almost custodial care of Joy. She would carry Joy and sing to her or talk to her but something seemed lacking in this. And then there was the time when a neighbor saw Paula at the park talking on her cell phone while Joy sat in the stroller. Brigit began to worry that Joy was missing out – on the joy of life she wanted her to have.

Nothing seemed right and no one seemed right.

10 COMMON MISPERCEPTIONS

I've identified 10 common misperceptions that can trip parents up during a nanny search. These are assumptions parents make based on a set of expectations mistakenly applied to a nanny search, which are easily made because they are so common and frequently passed along. Perhaps you have heard them before. If so, don't be so quick to buy into them, as they can fool you into making a wrong decision. Here they are—the assumptions and the reality behind them.

1. The Smoke-and-Mirrors Syndrome

The Assumption: "20 years' experience with kids means 20 years of good experience with kids." If you've cared for young children many times before, you certainly know what you're doing.

The Reality: Experience is not always informed, knowledgeable and relevant experience. Regardless of the quality of the résumé, you must ask tough questions of every candidate.

The "Smoke and Mirrors" assumption is fueled by a pervading sense that maternal instinct is universal. Women are born with an intrinsic ability to nurture and the knowledge required to care for children. Not only does caring for children come naturally, but the ability to do it right comes naturally as well.

When women choose to do the work of caring for children and have done it over time, it is not too far a leap to expect that they have honed their craft to perfection. Why question what comes naturally and the practice-makes-perfect model we hold so dear? Inevitably, the smoke clears. We recognize again and again that knowing how children develop and what skills are needed to properly care for them is neither instinctual nor universal. Perhaps we see children hitting someone else and the woman responsible for them pays no attention. Perhaps we see a toddler wandering around without supervision while the adult talks on her cell phone. These are the situations that shake our assumptions about maternal instinct. We are faced with the reality often, but we want to believe otherwise. We want the best for kids.

When hiring a nanny, maternal instinct often prevails. Our wish that a nanny will be naturally nurturing and that her experience has led to competence can be so strong that we can overlook the reality that the quality of her experience and skills is less than adequate.

2. I Can't Afford Quality

The Assumption: "All the good nannies work for rich families. You get what you pay for. If you pay more, you get better."

The Reality: Nannies value the support, respect and recognition parents provide more than an above-market salary. You don't need to offer more than market rate to hire a good nanny.

This assumption that all the good nannies work for rich families comes out of childhood stories about the lives of British aristocrats who raised a brood of children with help from a doting nanny. Our belief about a Mary Poppins from the last century comes alive in the present as we peek yet again into the lives of the rich and famous. Whether it's *The Nanny Diaries* or news briefs about the latest celebrity couple traveling with their nanny and children, we expect that only the rich get the best nannies, leaving the rest of the nannies to those unglamorous souls treading through a daily life of diapers and dishes who offer them a pittance of glory and market wages.

Does the "more you pay, the better you get" rule apply in the nanny market? Is compensation an indicator of quality? Assuming nannies are compensated fair market wages, asking whether the rich get all the good nannies misses the point. It may be more useful to turn the question around and ask, "Is compensation the only thing that motivates a nanny?" Just as in any type of employment, nannies have their own motivation to work in their profession. For some nannies, it is money or the excitement of being part of the lives of the rich and famous. Others find satisfaction in working with families that are less formal or on-the-go; with children who have a special need; or with children of a particular age group or ethnicity. Although these are not mutually exclusive, there is a primary motivating factor that influences a nanny to take a position with a particular family.

3. I Just Want a Babysitter

The Assumption: "All she's doing is watching my kids. My nanny's responsibility is making sure the kids are busy and not getting into trouble."

The Reality: Nannies create relationships with the children they care for. Whether the nanny is giving instruction, setting limits, negotiating or expressing feelings, a child will have a reaction.

Relationships are an important part of a child's understanding of the world and warrant attention. The perception that a nanny is someone who just watches the kids so they don't get into trouble involves a fair amount of parental denial. It can be a lot easier to assume this stranger is just watching the kids than to acknowledge she is creating a relationship with the kids and that this relationship has meaning over time. Even the babysitter who regularly comes once a month for date night is creating a relationship with the children.

It takes some work for parents to acknowledge what they are doing when hiring a nanny and coming to terms with their worries or concerns. For some, denial offers an easy out. Devaluing the relationship between a nanny and child, relegating her to being a babysitter who just watches the kids, becomes the solution.

4. Our Nanny Should Be Perfect in Every Way

The Assumption: "Our nanny loves our family and will do anything for us."

The Reality: While nannies often do love the families they work for, they also have personal lives outside of their working lives. This needs to be respected and supported.

The wish for the "be-all-and-end-all" nanny, who comes to a couple's door just when they need her, takes care of their kids whenever they need help, and works without ever complaining or ever leaving, is quite prevalent. What parent wouldn't want such nurturing, loving, attentive and self-sacrificing care from another!

Every reasonable parent recognizes that the wish for Mary Poppins is unrealistic. And yet the wish prevails, and it indicates the power of the human desire to be cared for. It is not merely a wish for the baby to be nurtured; the wish is that Mary Poppins will also nurture the parents. It is the parents' need for someone to reassure them, to lend a helping hand with the household chores, to know what the children need without having to be told and to be cheerfully available whenever needed.

5. One Size Fits All

The Assumption: "She was great with Mary's family, so she'll be great with us. Since we like Mary and her family, her nanny will certainly fit right into our family life."

The Reality: Your family may be different from your friend's in ways you aren't aware of, so don't make assumptions. It's better to ask the tough questions and also be prepared for the nanny's preference to work for a different type of family.

It can be a couple's dream come true when their neighbor's nanny is ready to start working with a new family just at the time they need help! They've seen the nanny care lovingly for their neighbor's child in the most challenging situations. They've observed her in the park and at the supermarket when she didn't know she was being watched. They've always said, "If only she could be our nanny!" And here that wish comes true. How fortunate!

These serendipitous situations are not always ready-made. Nannies may want to work in a different situation or have changing expectations for their next family. Parents may realize after meeting with the nanny that she is not the best match for them after all.

The assumption that our neighbor or friend's nanny will be the right match for us speaks to our deepest need to trust our nanny and our wish that the person we hire is not a stranger to us. What a relief from these intense worries if our nanny was known over time by a family we knew and trusted! Most certainly if they trusted her to care for the most important person in their life, then the nanny could be trusted with ours.

Most certainly if we like the parents and they saw eye-to-eye with their nanny, then their ideal match would be ours also. When these hopes are dashed, parents feel disappointed not only that their dream nanny isn't a fit, but also because their expectations about needing the same thing as their neighbors turned out to be false.

6. The Yo-Yo Effect

The Assumption: "Our last nanny was young and she didn't work out, so I'll get someone older this time. I should have seen this one coming, but I won't be so easily fooled the next time around!"

The Reality: Look a little closer. What is it about the fact that she was young that made her not work out?

There are many reasons why a parent hires a particular nanny. All parents want the best for their child and try to make the best decision they can about whom to hire. But misunderstandings and disappointments do happen in spite of the best of intentions. At times issues can be resolved, and everyone is generally better off for having gone through the situation and gotten out of it intact. At other times, things never get back on course and nannies have to leave.

While there's relief when an unfavorable situation is resolved, endings can shake up parents' sense of what they want in a nanny and their use of judgment. Perhaps they ignored their gut feelings that said she was not the right fit. Perhaps the choice of a nanny was right for the parents but not for the children. Perhaps the parents don't know what went wrong. They cling to anything for an answer. She was young—so get an older person the next time. She was not educated—so get someone with a college degree the next time. Her English was not fluent—so get a native English speaker the next time.

When parents start grasping at straws, it's a sign of just how desperate they are to regain confidence in their judgment. While the obvious can be true, better to look a little closer and ask further questions. Dig deeper.

What specifically was it about her youth or language skills or other characteristics that made her not work out? The answers will give you good data points to use in judging your next round of nanny candidates.

7. The Percentage Effect

The Assumption: "She'll do 70 percent housecleaning and 30 percent childcare, so I'll get a good house cleaner." The idea is to place the most emphasis on the main skill required for the position.

The Reality: While your housekeeper's duties include a considerable amount of cleaning, your child's care takes precedent. Make certain she also has good, solid childcare experience.

We live in a world of numbers. They provide a sense of security that all is in order in a changing environment. If you follow the numbers, you are in charge of uncertainty. Numbers rule! If the candidate will do 70 percent housekeeping and 30 percent childcare, it is easily assumed the search should focus on a candidate's housecleaning skills with less emphasis on childcare.

In this situation, numbers don't rule. What is more important when something goes wrong? If your housekeeper breaks a dish, you can more easily repair or replace it than if she harms your child. There are many excellent housekeepers who care responsibly for children as needed and as part of their housekeeping duties.

8. My Child Knows Best

The Assumption: "If my toddler says he hates her and wants her to go away, then she goes!" The belief is that the child uses good judgment and can be objective about who he wants taking care of him.

The Reality: Children can have many motivations for wanting a nanny to go away. Among them is wishing for their parent to stay home instead. Remember: you are the parent and the decision-maker.

When parents evaluate a nanny candidate, they often consider how she was when she first met their child. Did she pick up the baby right away? Was she loving, warm and interested in him? Was she playful with their toddler? Could she have an easy conversation with their preschooler? Parents also watch their child's reaction closely. Did the baby calm down when she held him? Did he go to her right away and enjoy playing with her? When she left, did he say he liked her?

While these observations and evaluations are important, it is equally important to factor in that nannies and children know they are being watched. The simple fact of being observed can affect behavior. Sometimes the message beneath the behavior merits more attention than the behavior itself. If a child says the nanny must go, then should the nanny go?

When it comes to the nanny hiring decision, parents know best. There are definitely mismatches between nannies and children, but the shoe is on the wrong foot when the child makes the decision about whom to hire.

9. Not Trusting Your Gut

The Assumption: "My gut says something doesn't feel right even though everything else seems okay . . ." Can anyone rely on gut feelings or hunches to make important decisions?

The Reality: When it comes to the complex decision about hiring a stranger to care for a child, parents who rely on both their gut feelings and the objective facts make more informed, better hiring decisions.

For centuries, philosophers advised against relying on gut feelings or hunches, widely considered idiosyncratic, unscientific and therefore unreliable. More recent evidence, however, suggests otherwise. In the past decade, research among neuroscientists has shown that intuition is useful and often indispensable when humans tackle complex and uncertain problems. Successful people are adept at judging the emotional experience of others, observing the nuances of their choices and the emotional consequences of their actions.

What these gut feelings may be saying is simply, "As wonderful as this nanny seems to be, she is not right for me." When a gut feeling is strong and persists, trust it and move on! Don't spin your wheels. Trying to put words to it can be futile. Parents who don't heed these warning signs eventually will discover what didn't feel right about their choice.

There is also another possibility. If a parent's gut feelings rule out every candidate and no candidate feels right, these feelings may be saying, "I don't want to hire a nanny! I want to take full responsibility at this time in my life to care for my child." Trust your gut instincts. Deciding not to hire a nanny could be a favorable outcome for you.

10. I'll Get Started Tomorrow

The Assumption: "There's still plenty of time to do this." Finding a nanny will be an easy and straightforward process.

The Reality: Expect to take four to six weeks to go through the process.

Some people tend to set short deadlines. They find something thrilling about having so much to do with very little time and so much at stake. There are others who tend to procrastinate. They like to put off until later what they can avoid doing in the present. If you fall into either camp, find support with friends and family to get started early. The process can take four to six weeks from start to finish.

As you go through your nanny search, and again as you're building a relationship with your new nanny, check this list from time to time to make sure you're not falling into any of these traps and making assumptions about your nanny that aren't realistic and will undermine both the search process and the ongoing relationship. You may be surprised to learn that you have some preconceived notions you didn't know you held.

GETTING YOUR
HEART IN GEAR

As I said in the introduction, this book is about using your heart, your soul and your mind to make one of the most important decisions you'll ever face. Encouraging and watching parents as they "get their hearts in gear" is some of the most rewarding work I do. It's a very personal part of the nanny search, and no two people are alike in terms of how they come to grips with their feelings.

How you respond to the idea of hiring a nanny is unique to you. What you feel and how intensely you feel it is idiosyncratic to you—your character, temperament and previous life experiences. Some moms approach this hiring decision quite pragmatically. It's a project with goals, objectives and a timeline. Other moms fret and worry long before doing anything. And yet uncharacteristically, a pragmatic mom might find herself unable to make a decision about whom to hire. Parents can meet a candidate with an impressive portfolio, strong letters of recommendation and a long history of caring for children. Their head says, "She matches up beautifully with everything I want in a nanny. She's great—don't pass her up!" And yet their heart says, "There's something about her I don't like." Although these parents may try to put words to their hunch that something isn't right, articulating why may not come easily. They are torn between making an important decision either with their head (based on objective criteria) or with their heart (based on a hunch). Choosing the latter can seem foolish by comparison. Perhaps no one seems right, in spite of meeting far too many candidates. Yet a mom who frets and worries may fall in love with her next-door neighbor's nanny and have the good fortune of her being available just when needed. Every mom's process and feelings are unique.

At the same time, there is some universality in the types of feelings mothers experience. It's quite expected that these will run the gamut from anticipation to worry, guilt, trepidation and relief. You may find your emotions come up unexpectedly and intensely, or that they are undefinable. Something just doesn't seem or feel right.

These feelings, however intense or known they may be, define a predictable set of worries that are part of the process of hiring and partnering with a nanny. I call them the Five Heartfelt Worries About Hiring a Nanny. These are worries about being able to trust a stranger, being replaced as a mom, feeling inadequate as a mom, feeling guilty because you're hiring someone to do your job or feeling jealous of the nanny you hire.

The Five Heartfelt Worries

1. Trust

Every parent worries and wants to be certain his or her child is safe and nurtured. If parents *didn't* worry about their child's safety and care, it would be a major cause for concern. Yet, as Dr. Stern noted and as most moms eventually recognize, at some point in their child's young life a parent needs to separate for a variety of reasons.[18] When this time comes, a mom has to have enough confidence to leave her child

---

18   Daniel N. Stern, M.D., *The Birth of a Mother: How the Motherhood Experience Changes You Forever* (New York: Basic Books, 1998).

in the care of a responsible adult. If this adult is a known and trusted person, the experience of leaving can be a positive one. Admittedly, though, hiring a nanny doesn't come with a built-in level of trust. Often the nanny is someone a parent has known for only a brief period of time. How much does a parent need to know about a nanny to trust she would act responsibly?

Over the years, I have come to realize that parents use what I call a "healthy sense of denial" when they leave their child in the care of someone they have known for only a short time. It is healthy because they know "enough" to trust she will do no harm, and it is "denial" because they can't really know "enough" in such a short period to trust her completely.

The media fans the fires that burn under a mom's worries about trust. How can a mom ignore the reality that horrible things happen to responsible mothers who trusted their nanny? In the court of public opinion, these mothers are often blamed as much as the nanny who committed the horrific crime. How, the media cries, could this mother be so irresponsible, so naïve and so trusting?

In October 2012, Yoselyn Ortega, a 50-year-old nanny from the Dominican Republic, was accused of the murder of two children in her care, then six and two years old, whom she had cared for since the elder child was 18 months old. The incident went viral on the internet and reignited the most heart-wrenching worry a mother has: "Can I trust my child will be safe in the care of my nanny? Can I trust what I know about this woman? What goes on when I'm not around?" Among the commentaries and condolences to the mother of the murdered children, some blamed her, holding her accountable for her nanny's actions. If this mother had been more attentive or less demanding, the nanny would have been less stressed; if this mother had paid her more, the nanny wouldn't have had trouble with finances. These accusations and ready-made solutions rang true for some mothers who—beyond what is expected in an employer-employee relationship—voluntarily gave their nanny a loan to get out of debt, purchased a car for the nanny or paid for the education of their nanny's children. They took care of their nanny as an insurance policy, a safety net to guarantee their children would be safe, and to assuage guilt and cushion fears.[19]

2. Being Replaced

Some parents imagine their child running to their nanny for comfort or even calling her "Mommy," and they want to stop the nanny-hiring process immediately. They imagine the long hours they may be away from home and their children curling up with their nanny at nap time because they miss their mom. These thoughts can simply break a mother's heart, which then spills into a big worry. If your child spends more time during his waking hours with their nanny than he does with you, are you being replaced? Is your nanny taking your place as mother to your child? Reassurances from others can feel like empty words falling on a heavy heart. A well-intentioned friend could say, "Of course you're the mom! All kids know who their mom is." Or, "Children say things they don't mean—it's only a word she's using. She doesn't mean your nanny is her mom!"

---

19   Ollie Gillman, "Nanny accused of stabbing two young children to death 'because their parents asked her to do more work around their Upper West Side apartment' appears in court looking gaunt and frail," Daily Mail.com, October 9, 2015.

CARMEN'S STORY

Carmen, a nanny with over 20 years' experience, described the elephant in the room in the mother-nanny relationship: "Mothers usually feel jealous of nannies. They worry, 'Here's Carmen and she's all day every day with my baby. She feeds him, cleans up after him, changes his dirty diapers, carries him and sings to him.' One of the children I took care of was named Michael. One night, Michael woke up crying and sick, and all he said was, 'Carmen, I want Carmen.' His mother couldn't calm him down, so she called me and asked me what to do. In the morning she said she was relieved I could help that night. But I know what she really wanted to say was, 'Why do I have to call you? Why shouldn't my son be crying for me to help him feel better?'"

3. Inadequacy

Am I a good parent? This worry is an expectable response for first-time moms. One of the realities for many new parents is that they are learning on the job. New parents are often "entry-level status," some never having changed a diaper before or given a bottle to a hungry baby. When faced with other more complex requirements, such as establishing feeding and sleeping routines, setting limits or teaching children how to get along with each other, many first-time parents need mentoring and a little advice from someone they trust.

The question about adequacy is not only the domain of first-time parents! At various times, most parents are challenged throughout the life span of their child as to whether they have used good judgment or wished in retrospect that they would have done something differently.

This can pose a dilemma when hiring a nanny. On the one hand, you may want advice from your nanny. On the other, you don't want to be upstaged by a competent nanny who makes you feel like you're just treading water.

You want advice and yet you want to be in charge. You want to minimize errors of judgment while getting a reprieve for those you create. You want to be, as Winnicott[20] has eloquently defined, a "good-enough parent." Most of all, you certainly don't want to be overshadowed by your competent nanny in the eyes of your child.

20　D. W. Winnicott, *The Child, the Family and the Outside World* (London: Penguin, 1973), 173.

4. Guilt

If you find it difficult to hand over responsibility to someone else, guilt may well find its way into your nanny relationship. If you are a perfectionist and need to be certain whatever you do is at the 100-percent level, guilt will almost certainly interfere with being a good-enough parent.[21]

Feelings of guilt are often learned at an early age. They can be reinforced through family rituals and traditions, and within social and cultural systems. They are not easily undone. They often serve a common good and teach meaningful values such as the Golden Rule or a strong work ethic. When it comes to parenting, a healthy amount of guilt keeps parents on the job. Too much guilt, however, can keep a parent in such a state of worry or conversely in denial that it's difficult to do a good-enough job.

There's a lot that mothers can feel guilty about. One is hiring a nanny. You may feel guilty because you can't do it all without her. You may feel guilty because you have a nanny and aren't managing her well enough. You may feel guilty because you hired a good-enough nanny and not the best nanny. You may feel guilty because you truly know you can't be 100 percent at both work and at parenting—that balancing work and family is a frustrating and continuous process.

5. Envy or Jealousy

Parents often experience sharp pangs of jealousy when they learn their nanny experienced an event with their child that they wish they'd had, such as their child's first step or rolling over for the first time. They may feel envy when the nanny tells an animated story about the fun she and the child had together. Why does the nanny get all the "goodies" while the parent works?

---

21 Ibid.

Faced with the reality that her nanny will spend more hours per day with her child than she will, many a mother has created an accounting system recording hours-spent-with-nanny versus hours-spent-with-mom. If the numbers don't balance, a quality-versus-quantity time measurement is implemented. Quality time spent with her child is more meaningful than a lot of "empty" time. Whatever the outcome of this number crunching, the reality for many mothers is that they constantly scan their child for any signs that they are coming in second place, or having their mothering moments taken away by a competent nanny. These signs often appear unexpectedly, such as when seeing their child devour the homemade dinner the nanny had time to prepare, or while at work, imagining the pleasure of bath time with the child that evening, only to return home and find the nanny toweling off a freshly bathed child.

It may help assuage your fears to know that from a scientific and objective viewpoint, it is well documented that children know their parents. Research on infants and toddlers shows that children have the capacity to create complex, meaningful and individualized relationships with all the adults caring for them—in other words, they can differentiate parents from nanny. The relationship children create with their nanny will be different in unique ways from the relationship they have with their parents. Over time and through many experiences with their child, parents learn they can't be replaced in their rightful role as parents *and* that their child will have a relationship with the nanny that will be different from theirs.

Jeree H. Pawl, PhD, has reminded us that "Human relationships are the foundations upon which children build their future. All of the relationships that touch very young children are important."[22] Children learn within relationships about themselves and the world around them. Whether that relationship is the mother, father, grandparents, friend, neighbor or nanny, a child learns about who he is and how he is in relation to these adults. In fact, research has shown that children flourish when they have the opportunity to create close relationships with different caregivers.[23]

22   Zero to Three: National Center for Infants, Toddlers and Families, Jeree H. Pawl, PhD., Washington D.C. 1998, P. 3

23   https://www.childtrends.org/wp-content/uploads/2013/12/2013-54CaringAdults.pdf

PREPARING YOUR SOUL: A QUESTION OF VALUES

Chances are that ever since you knew you were going to be a mother, and probably even before that, you've been planning how you want to raise your child. You've been looking back on how you were raised and having discussions with your partner about how he or she was raised. Maybe you'll do things differently than your parents did and maybe some things you do will be the same. You both have hopes and dreams about the world you want your child to live in, what opportunities you want for your children and what decisions you want them to make to have a meaningful life. At the heart of those decisions are values.

What are values and how are they learned? Values are a person's principles or standards of behavior. They are one's judgment of what is important in life and how one sees and interacts with the world. They speak to the essence of who we are—our souls.

Values fall into various categories, including ethical, moral, religious, political, cultural, social and aesthetic. Individuals learn what values are important from their parents, family, community, the larger society and culture. As an example, in Western society, generally acceptable values include the Golden Rule—to treat others as you would treat yourself; the value of independence and autonomy; freedom of speech and privacy; respect for differences and equal rights regardless of race or gender.

When you search for a nanny, you want someone whose worldview aligns enough with yours that you know when you're not around, your children are being brought up with your family values in mind. Most parents don't consider the importance of family values when hiring a nanny. Why would they be important when there are so many other factors to consider?

As each of us grows up, we form a system of values through interactions with others that share similar or conflicting values. As we endorse those that resonate and reject those we deem objectionable, we prioritize our set of values in order to make important decisions about our lives. During our teen years, autonomy and independence may hold high ranking as we navigate the emotional mine field of who we are and what makes meaningful work. As we move into the arena of creating ongoing intimate relationships, values often shift, allowing dependency to take precedent over autonomy. Regardless of changes over time, the core values that comprise our value system inform how we view the world, as well as the decisions we make about how we live our lives among others.

Becoming a parent is a time when values necessarily shift to accommodate the responsibility of caring for another human being. Along with the responsibility of ensuring the infant is nurtured and cared for comes the attendant responsibility of teaching the child values. Parents either consciously or unconsciously make decisions about what values to instill, but also in their daily interactions, make choices about how to teach these values.

It's only natural that nannies have their own value systems, rules of behavior and child-rearing practices based on past experiences from the culture and family they were raised in. Consciously or unconsciously, nannies bring their value systems into the relationship they create with you and your child. And the more these value systems are acknowledged between you and your nanny, the greater likelihood your child will grow up learning a consistent set of values about what is important in life and what the expectations are to support these values.

This is not to say parents and nannies need to have the same worldview. Clearly differences can be healthy! Whether you have different views on politics, religion, the relative importance of dependency compared with independence, etc., what is most essential is to understand those differences and decide how you will navigate them with your nanny.

SKITTLES'S STORY

"Where did our dog go when he died?" Iris's best buddy was her Cavalier King Charles spaniel, Skittles. When she and Scott married, Skittles marched down the aisle in a custom-made tuxedo to the delight of all their guests! It was just as it should have been. After all, Skittles was "family." When David was born, Skittles became his four-legged big brother: patient, playful and never complaining about his ears and tail getting pulled. As the years went by, Skittles and David became best buddies, hanging out playing blocks or chasing around the dog park. Over time, Skittles lost his desire and ability to run and chase. Rosario, David's nanny, would gently remind David that Skittles was getting old and needed to rest. Out of the blue, David said, "When people get old, they die. Where do dogs go when they die?" "They go to dog heaven, of course," Rosario simply said. But it wasn't so simple. That night, David proudly passed this newly discovered information to his parents. Iris and Scott were not so delighted. "We are Jewish," Iris noted, "and Jews don't believe there is a heaven."

Values and Stereotypes

When differences are out in the open, it's an opportunity to teach children the value of accepting individual differences and respecting others for their views. The challenge in doing this comes from differences that are not made explicit, whether because they are unconscious or consciously kept from view. These implicit biases and the cultural and racial stereotypes formed find their way into both the hiring process and the nanny-parent relationship.

Every parent wants to hire someone who is honest, trustworthy, loving and experienced. Additional characteristics include patience and kindness, as well as being active, playful, upbeat, easygoing, fun, nurturing, warm and motivated. There's a wide body of evidence showing how certain characteristics and traits associated with cultural and racial stereotypes influence hiring practices.[24] This is the slippery slope that can catch a well-intentioned parent off guard. You want someone who is warm, nurturing, kind and loving? Hire a Latina or a Tibetan nanny! You want someone smart and educated, with a strong work ethic? Hire a college graduate! You want someone family-oriented, honest and stable? Hire a nanny from the rural Midwest!

In addition to differences in held values (the hiring decisions based on unconscious stereotypes), there can be cultural differences in child-rearing that underlie how a parent and a nanny manage behaviors in young children in order to teach similar values. For example, take the observed practices in different cultures around how to help infants establish the daily routines of feeding, sleeping and playing. These practices range from the Westernized method of "crying it out" to an "on demand" method practiced in third-world countries. How easy is it for a nanny from a rural area of Thailand who nursed her own

---

24   http://blogs.wsj.com/atwork/2013/01/10/how-racial-stereotypes-may-influence-hiring-for-top-jobs/

children "on demand" while carrying them on her back to get her American employer's baby on a schedule by letting him "cry it out"? What deeply held values is she implicitly compromising by doing so? Similar challenges occur in the area of discipline. While some Western practices adhere to a "time-out" method, other cultures insist that time out is a form of punishment. They may believe that tantrums should be managed by the group, teaching a child what the group norm is for acceptable behavior.

MAE'S STORY

Mae huddled outside the baby's room, her eyes glued to the clock as it ticked away the minutes. How much longer would she have to endure the baby's crying? It broke her heart and her spirit to do this but she was not the mother, she was the nanny. Marianne had explained how important it was to let the baby cry for 10 minutes before going into the room and picking him up. She said it was teaching her baby to learn to sleep on his own. She said she wanted her baby to learn to be independent. Somehow Mae didn't understand the logic. Mae was born and raised in a small, rural village in Thailand. When her babies were born, until they learned to walk, Mae carried them on her back. When they cried, she moved them to the front and nursed them. At night, the babies slept next to her so when they cried Mae could sing to them, rock them and nurse them until they went back to sleep. Mae thought, "My children are independent. Why do we have to let babies cry alone to teach them independence?"

As you prepare to move forward with your nanny search, remember that there is bound to be something you and your nanny disagree on. When differences occur, look for the value you each want to teach the child. While what you choose to do may not change, it can be helpful to identify, understand and respect differences in values or in how you teach a similar value.

PUTTING YOUR WORRIES IN PERSPECTIVE: A SUCCESS STORY

The big, heartfelt concern about "Am I doing right by my child?" is one that really doesn't go away. Sure, there are times when the way your nanny is caring for your child feels perfectly aligned with the universe and the concerns about doing "right" fall off your worry list. How could you have given this so much energy and airtime?

This was Janice and Joe's experience. Their boys were now seven and nine years old and Sylvia, their nanny, had been part of their family since their first son was born. The boys were thriving in all the ways they had hoped for. They were very closely attached to Sylvia, "joined at the hip" in many ways. She had raised them with all the values she had promised when they first met: the boys were respectful, smart, great in school and had lots of friends. Family time was pleasurable and fun. Janice and Joe felt their decision to be parents was the right one for them and that hiring Sylvia to be part of this journey was the right decision to make.

Then Sylvia had to leave, for reasons both personal—to take care of her new grandchild—and practical—the boys didn't need a nanny full-time and Sylvia didn't want to do the household chores. So this question "Am I doing right by my child?" reared its ugly head again after nine years of being off their worry list.

Janice and Joe peppered each other with questions. "Sure, we need to make the change, but how will we do this so we're not undoing all that went right so far? What if the person we choose is a disaster? Who is best for our boys now? How much of Sylvia's character is what we need? How much of who she wasn't do we want now?"

They created a summary of Sylvia pros and cons, along with a list of what work they needed done now and in the near future. They noted what the boys liked and didn't like about Sylvia. But what they couldn't list was what the boys wanted and didn't want in their new nanny.

Were the boys old enough to participate in this decision? How much of the decision-making should they give them? What was the value in having them participate at all?

Involving the boys ultimately knocked the "Am I doing right?" question right off the worry list. Here's what happened.

Janice and Joe knew their boys had their own ideas about what they wanted in their new nanny. They also knew the boys shouldn't make the decision about whom to hire. So the plan was to engage them in the initial part of the process to find out what they wanted, and then after initial interviews and before a trial with two candidates Janice and Joe selected as promising, engage the boys again. The boys could share their preferences but needed to know their parents would make the final decision.

The boys loved the idea! The discussion about what they wanted was tons of fun; it was a chance to reminisce, laugh and get serious about what they learned in their relationship with Sylvia. It was both familiar territory for Janice and Joe and not. Sure, the content of what the boys said about Sylvia wasn't unfamiliar; it was how thoughtful they were about their relationship with her that was unexpected. She had truly influenced the boys in ways Janice and Joe hadn't fully appreciated. If the boys could be as thoughtful about what they wanted and what they had experienced with Sylvia, then the decision about whom to hire would be well made.

And that's when they put the "Am I doing right?" question off their worry list for a while longer.

Three years later, it came up again. This time the relationship with the nanny they hired was a mixed bag of "like" and "dislike." Janice and Joe felt it and knew the boys did also. They knew everyone has their positive and negative attributes and the negatives weren't sufficiently bad to switch nannies; but when the opportunity arose to make a change, they didn't resist.

The boys were now 10 and 12 years old. They loved to analyze and debate. Chess was one of their favorite games. When Janice and Joe ramped up to find a new nanny, they decided to implement the process they had used previously, with an updated twist. In addition to discussing what the boys wanted based on current experience, they would make a list of the qualities and characteristics of their ideal nanny and then prioritize these. Janice and Joe would separately do this and together they would merge the lists. Before the trial, the boys created a list of what they would observe during their time with the prospective nanny to help their parents make a hiring decision. After the trial, the family would have a discussion about whom they wanted to hire based on observation and comment. As expected, Janice and Joe would make the final decision.

The process was amazingly rich with content and emotion. That was a powerful enough experience for Janice and Joe, but going through a process that taught their sons just how difficult it is to evaluate good human beings on their ability to perform work that is relationship-based was a game-changer for everyone. They knew their sons would make better employers in the future, but beyond that, better reflect their own character, self-worth and values in how they would treat others in the workplace. That was when the enduring question "Am I doing right?" once again came off their worry list for a while longer.

KNOW BEFORE YOU GO: PUTTING YOUR MIND INTO GEAR

Before we tackle the nuts and bolts of the hiring process, it's essential to be mentally prepared and know what to expect. This may not be an easy process, or a fast process for that matter. Deciding where to look, checking references, conducting interviews and wading through paperwork can be draining. Keep the end goal in mind and be patient. Investing time in advance to really think through what you want, what you need and what will work best for your family will pay off in the end.

KATE'S STORY PART I

Between her strong yet mixed emotions, her sleep deprivation and her imminent return to work, Kate was in somewhat of a fog. But she knew she needed to map out a childcare strategy—after all she was a successful businesswoman, so she could certainly handle this. Yet as she sat down with pen to paper while her baby was napping, she found that she had more questions than answers.

When to Start the Search

It may come as a surprise that it can take between four and six weeks to complete the hiring process. In most nanny searches, creating a job description and recruiting for viable candidates comprises the first week or longer. Initial and second interviews follow during the second and third weeks. This leaves two to three weeks to check references, further evaluate candidates, make decisions about whom to hire, go through a trial period and get agreement on terms before your nanny makes her official start.

Some searches don't go smoothly. Your desired candidate may decide to take a position with another family or her references may not be reassuring. Perhaps the trial shows a nanny's lack of skills in an important area. In these situations and others, you'll need to restart the process.

A word to the wise: start on time! With such an important decision at stake, you don't want to be pressured to hire just anyone today because you need childcare tomorrow.

KATE'S STORY PART II

For the first month of her baby's life, Kate's time was consumed with getting to learn how a typical day would go. The feedings happened every two to three hours, and then there was the changing, cuddling, cooing, observing and simply loving the time she spent with her baby. Then it was time to sleep for an hour or so—and soon the next feeding would start. Of course, there were days when the baby was fussy and everything was "off." There was no real routine to her day. Although she was exhausted, for the most part, Kate was loving every crazy minute of it.

The maternity leave clock truly didn't appear on her radar until a month after delivery. Three months seemed like forever. Then the second month came and went. Imagining going back to work began to haunt the busy days and with very mixed feelings, she looked at the calendar—only two weeks before she was expected back at work! She knew financially that she needed to return to work, and part of her wanted to go. But the other part of her couldn't imagine leaving her. Did she really need to find someone to take care of this new love in her life so soon?

Know What You Need

Before you jump in, take the time to consider what type of childcare arrangement you really need. Do you need overnight assistance with a newborn? Help with the kids and housework a few mornings a week? A live-in nanny? Remember that one type of nanny does not fit all families. In fact, there are nine types of nannies and five types of nanny arrangements. When considering what is best for your family at this time in their life, it's important to think broadly and look ahead. Often parents are focused on their immediate childcare needs and neglect to give their search a wider, long-term perspective. Most families need more than one nanny to cover those situations when their child is sick or when their nanny is sick or on vacation. Others need a nanny for evenings and weekends. Having a list of one or two nannies who could cover these situations is important. It's also essential to consider your future childcare needs. Most families will require some form of childcare assistance for the first five years of their children's lives until they begin a full day at elementary school. Many more need childcare support for the after-school hours throughout the elementary school years.

MARY'S STORY

On one of those rainy San Francisco days with both kids running around the house, Mary felt trapped. She also felt resentful. She was cranky and short with the kids. She felt like the bad she had most wanted not to become.

Mary knew she needed a break from the kids. A couple of days a week for a few hours would make the difference. She envisioned going for a walk alone along the water or having an uninterrupted conversation over lunch with a friend. She knew on this most terrible of days, a short break would be the best for her and for the kids. Mary didn't want a full-charge nanny. She didn't need someone to take on a lot of the responsibilities for the girls. She just needed someone who could provide some respite.

Nine Types of Childcare Providers

1. Nanny: Provides full-charge childcare, either full-time or part-time, with both parents working inside or outside the home.

2. Mother's Helper: Works alongside a stay-at-home parent, assisting in managing both the care of the children and the household.

3. Family Assistant: Provides household support to parents, allowing the parents to focus on caring for their children. A family assistant also provides a combination of household support when a child is in school and then after-school care until the parent returns home.

4. Au Pair: A non-U.S.-born person between the ages of 18 and 26 years old who immigrates to the U.S. on a U.S. Government–issued visa to provide up to 40 hours per week of childcare. In return, the au pair receives a small stipend, room/board and the cultural experience of living with an American family for one year, with the option to extend to two years.

5. Post-partum Doula: Specializes in the care of newborns and provides support to the parents and care for the newborn up to four months of age on a flexible schedule, including nights.

6. Newborn Care Specialist: A specialist trained and skilled in newborn care. She provides expertise in all aspects of newborn care, parental education and support.

7. Housekeeper: Provides housecleaning services primarily, but also as-needed childcare when the parent or nanny is not available to do so.

8. Babysitter: An individual who provides as-needed childcare, generally on evenings and weekends. Many babysitters are middle school, high school or college age, although some adults provide babysitting as well.

8. Special Needs Therapist: A licensed, qualified clinician who provides therapeutic services to a child with special needs in collaboration with the parents and other professionals.

9. Tutor: An individual with expertise in certain subject areas who provides guidance or instruction in a specific academic subject.

Five Types of Childcare Arrangements

1. Live-Out: The nanny comes to the family's home to perform her duties.

2. Live-In: The nanny lives in the family's home. Some families hire a nanny to live in their home for their scheduled workdays, returning to their own families on their days off.

3. Share Care: Two or more families partner to hire a nanny who provides care for children in either one or both of the families' homes. Families share responsibility equally for the compensation/benefits and support given to the nanny. Share care is also an arrangement when a nanny brings her own child and provides care for both children.

4. Staffed Household: Childcare is provided by more than one nanny to ensure 60-plus hours per week of childcare, including seven days per week of coverage.

5. Co-op: Two or more families share the care of all children in one or more of the families' homes, swapping days or hours with each other in a mutually determined, fair arrangement.

Scheduling

Determine the hours and days you need childcare. You may want to add 15 to 20 minutes to your nanny's schedule at the beginning and/or end of the day for debriefing. Other factors to consider include:

1. Flexibility: Some parents routinely run late getting home because of traffic or last-minute meetings at work and need someone who can stay later on a short notice.

2. Changing schedule: Some parents have an unpredictable schedule and need someone with flexibility to adjust the hours and days worked.

3. Travel: Do you need someone who will travel with you for family vacations or business trips? If so, how often and for how long? How much notice can you provide?

4. Overnight care: Do you need someone to stay in your home overnight when you are traveling for personal or business reasons? If so, how many nights will you be away and how much notice would you provide?

Responsibilities

The following is a list of duties associated with in-home childcare. While these duties are industry standard, they should not be assumed. They should be listed on the job description and discussed in detail during interviews. You will also want to list and discuss any special needs your family may have, such as administering medications.

1. Nanny: *Childcare:* Feeding, changing, bathing, transporting the children to and from school or activities, providing safe and developmentally appropriate activities, meal preparation. Responsibilities that are not standard but could be included as agreed on by both parties: laundry and meal preparation for the family.

Light Housecleaning: Child's room kept clean, toys clean and put away, bed linens clean and put away, child's bed changed and clean, child's laundry washed, dried, folded and put away. Nanny cleans up after herself and the child, keeping the house in the same order it is usually kept.

Errands: As needed to pick up groceries, dry cleaning, post office, etc.

2. Mother's helper: Responsibilities are the same as for nanny in partnership with the parent and include weekly grocery shopping, meal preparation and laundry for the family.

3. Babysitter: Responsibilities are mutually determined to include all or part of the standard responsibilities above.

What Do You Want: The Ideal Relationship for You

There can be several ways of thinking about the type of relationship you want to have with your nanny. Perhaps you want someone to take the reins and make decisions while you're at work. Others prefer to work more collaboratively with their nanny, with the nanny consulting them on decisions and situations as they arise. Giving thought to this in advance will help you choose a nanny who fits with the relationship style you need.

KATE'S STORY PART III

It was a challenge for Kate to know what kind of relationship she would want with her nanny. Being an employer/mom hiring an employee/nanny raised certain questions she hadn't thought of before. How would she manage her nanny and how much did she want to manage her? Did she imagine their relationship would be formal or collegial? Would she want to feel like friends, like family or like a manager with her nanny?

Full-charge Executive

You are a working mother who enjoys her career—you don't like distractions at work. You want a nanny who will take charge, who calls you only if there is a true emergency. She'll convey important information at the end of the day, but she can handle most situations without your input. This is a nanny who knows what she's doing and can take full responsibility for the schedules, care and management of your children. This type of nanny requires no hand-holding from you and will be completely self-sufficient.

Collaborator

You are a working mother who enjoys her career but wants to raise her children in partnership with a childcare provider. You want to form a close relationship with the nanny to ensure that you're working together to give your children the kind of care and attention they need. Each day, she arrives a few minutes early and leaves a few minutes late so you can talk about the children and share any important details about their day. She texts you often with pictures and comments about your child's day with her. Sometimes you FaceTime or video chat over Skype together. She's invited to your child's birthday parties and family holiday events.

Supporter

You prefer a nanny who is experienced and takes direction from you about the care of the children. You want your nanny to be knowledgeable and trustworthy, and to share very similar values and child-rearing orientations. You want to be in charge of development, planning the activities and decisions about care, then delegating these to your nanny to implement.

Helper/Intern

You want a nanny who is younger and less skilled but who is eager to learn and loves being with children. In these relationships, moms often mentor their nannies, teaching them how to manage the daily routines, discipline problems, etc., while the nannies bring fresh, youthful and dynamic interest to the relationships.

A Worthy Comment:

Relationships between parents and nannies are not always a partnership. They can be degrading, exploitative or in extreme cases, emotionally or physically abusive. These unhealthy relationships are illustrated in films, such as the recent movie The Help[25], in popular literature, such as The Nanny Diaries[26], and in the socio-feminist writings of Cameron Macdonald, author of Shadow Mothers[27]. While allowing for the freedom of expression and artistic creativity found in these stories, sadly these relationships do exist outside the realm of fiction, to a greater or lesser degree, in the ordinary lives of mothers and nannies, and this fact should give us pause.

It is not the intent of this book to dwell on those situations when parents and nannies abuse trust placed in each other. Rather, the intent is to bring to the foreground the complexity of the parent-nanny relationship.

All relationships navigate the balance of power based on a variety of factors. These include economic disparity and racial and cultural prejudices. Another is individual character and temperament. It is important to acknowledge that when the power balance shifts to being harmful and cruel, this type of relationship is neither a healthy partnership nor one that is in the best interests of the child.

---

25 *The Help*, Touchstone Pictures, Walt Disney Movie Studios, August 20, 2011. https://en.wikipedia.org/wiki/The_Help_(film)

26 Emma McLaughlin and Nicola Kraus, *The Nanny Diaries: A Novel* (New York: St. Martin's Griffin, 2002).

27 Cameron Macdonald, *Shadow Mothers: Nannies, Au Pairs, and the Micropolitics of Mothering* (Berkeley: University of California Press, 2010).

What Do You Wish For: The Ideal Relationship for Your Child

I've found it best to ask parents, "If the ideal candidate came into your home today, who would that person be? What is it about her that would make her seem so ideal?"

For some parents it is Mary Poppins or Mrs. Doubtfire. For others it is someone they know. You might find yourself saying, "If only my mom could be my nanny, life would be so easy!" or "If only my best friend could do this, I would feel so reassured!" Equally important is identifying people you could not imagine as your nanny. What is it about these people that makes them less than ideal?

Here's an example of how one characteristic, age, factors into a parent's wish list. Most parents attribute certain characteristics to chronological age, such as maturity, stamina and activity level. Age also affects the relationship parents have with their nanny. If the nanny is contemporary in age with the parents, the relationship may be different—more like a colleague or friend—than with an older nanny, who may be more like a "grandmother" to the children, or a younger one, who may be more like a "big sister" to the children.

A Maternal Nurturer for Baby and You

If this is your first child, chances are you're equal parts enamored with and terrified about the prospect of being responsible for another human life. You've read books about parenting and prepared yourself the best you can, but at the end of the day, what if something goes wrong? You wish your mother lived nearby, but she's several states away. You decide to focus your nanny search on someone older—a nanny who has extensive experience with newborns and new mothers.

A Social, Active Teacher for Baby and You

She may be your age or slightly older, and she is active, creative and playful with your children and interested in sharing her years of experience with you. She creates age-appropriate games, takes the children to neighborhood activities and strives to work together in a partnership with you to ensure the children are constantly engaged and learning new things in the world around them.

A Big Sister/Role Model

A young, energetic nanny who your children can look up to may be the ideal candidate for your family. Maybe she grew up taking care of younger siblings or cousins, so even though she's young, she has ample experience with children. She's a pro at creating fun and imaginative activities. The kids see her as an awesome adult and can't wait to spend time with their new "big sister."

A Fun-loving Occasional Playmate for Child and Date Night Minder for You

Maybe she comes only once a week or once a month, but it's important to have someone available when you need a date night or time to yourself. She meets all of your qualifications, she's available when you need her and the kids look forward to her visits.

Remember, if you put in the legwork and stay the course, you'll eventually find a nanny who fits with your family's needs. What is right for someone else might not be right for you or your children. Once you've found the right nanny, you'll realize your efforts were entirely worth it.

Are you ready? Let's get started on the process.

Eight Steps to Finding the Right Nanny for Your Family

I've compiled a list of the eight steps that most families go through during their nanny search and an overview of each step.

The Nanny Manual digs deeper into each area, but these brief descriptions should give you an idea of what to look for and the tools you'll need to compile for each step of the journey ahead.

1. Evaluation of Need

Determining your needs is the first step to any nanny search. How many hours do you want her to work? How will you handle the legal responsibilities you have with the various government agencies? What is your childcare budget? What qualities and characteristics do you want in your nanny? Do you want your nanny to do light housekeeping? Will she live in your home or need to travel with you? These and many more questions about your family's specific childcare needs must be answered before you can proceed to the next step.

2. Job Description

The job description is where you put your needs down on paper. Here, you'll not only list your requirements for the type of nanny arrangement you're looking for, you'll also state the legal, health and safety requirements you're looking for in a nanny, as well as list what you're offering for compensation and benefits, etc.

3. Advertising the Position

Once you've created your job description, you'll start to advertise to find candidates. Whether you post your advertisement on job boards such as Care.com or Craigslist, mother's groups or a neighborhood group listserv, a college job board or elsewhere, it's important that you include all the pertinent information to ensure you get responses from nannies who fit your qualifications.

4. Prescreening Candidates

Before you proceed to reference checking or interviews, a quick prescreen of the applicants is vital. Confirm the nanny is available during the days and times you requested, and review other areas including compensation, taxable income, documentation, etc. Then, if she meets your basic requirements, it's time to proceed.

5. Checking References

Checking references is an important part of the nanny search, as it provides insight into how the nanny has cared for children and how she has worked with parents in the past. However, remember that no two families are alike, and a nanny's experience with one family may be entirely different with another.

6. Interviewing

Once you've narrowed the field, it's time for in-person interviews. Generally, parents interview four or five candidates during round one, then call one candidate back for a second, less formal interview.

7. Trial

The trial period is generally a one-to-two-week period when the nanny works for your family (with pay) to determine if she is the right fit. You'll closely observe and train her during this time, and at the end of the trial, you'll offer her a contract if you feel she is the right choice for your family's needs.

8. The Contract

At the end of the trial period, you'll provide your nanny with a contract stating the agreed-upon terms to ensure there are no gray areas about either party's responsibilities moving forward.

THE NUTS AND BOLTS FOR A SUCCESSFUL NANNY SEARCH

• •

We all know the "devil is in the details," right? That is especially true when it comes to hiring a nanny. Before you begin your quest to find the right nanny for your family, it's important to familiarize yourself with the nuts and bolts of what you'll need to do to ensure the search goes smoothly.

Taxes

Parents have a responsibility to the Internal Revenue Service (IRS) when hiring a nanny. Nannies are considered hourly wage employees by the IRS, not subcontractors, and should be treated as employees. The 2016 IRS law on Household Employees requires that a parent who pays more than $2,000 per calendar year to a nanny withhold the 7.65 percent Social Security, Unemployment, Disability and Medicare taxes (FICA) on their nanny's salary. Additionally, parents are required to pay the nanny's 7.65 percent portion of FICA on a quarterly or year-end basis.

Parents may have other tax responsibilities, such as federal unemployment taxes and a variety of state taxes. A nanny chooses to pay her personal income taxes either on a regular basis through allocated W-2 withholdings or at year-end when she files her income tax return. While these taxes add to the initial cost of in-home childcare, there are several ways to offset your tax burden. These include taking pretax dollars from a flexible spending account (DeCAP) managed by your employer, a Childcare Tax Credit, and deducting medical insurance premiums, tuition costs, retirement savings and transportation expenses from your nanny's gross income. Please consult with your tax accountant for advice on the best vehicle to offset nanny taxes.

Parents who do not pay taxes on a nanny's salary incur the risk of paying penalties and interest on the unpaid taxes if audited by the IRS.

Take it from the street: You may have several acquaintances or heard about other parents who do not pay taxes on childcare. These families believe paying taxes increases the cost of care and reduces the pool of applicants, and a nanny payroll account can be cumbersome to set up and maintain. Many nannies have budgets based on earning nontaxable income and will accept a position if paid cash only. Some nannies will accept taxable income if parents pay the nanny's federal and state personal income taxes and the required FICA taxes. Some nannies request a part-taxable arrangement. It is very important that you make decisions about the nanny tax before you begin the hiring process. If you will compensate your nanny with all income taxed, this must be part of all announcements, as well as initial and ongoing discussions with your nanny candidates.

Overtime Laws

In 2016, the U.S. Department of Labor ruled that nannies are hourly wage employees and, as such, required to be paid overtime for all hours worked over nine hours per day and 40 hours per week. It is strongly recommended that parents pay attention to overtime rules and state in their Nanny Agreement what the under-40 hourly rate is and the overtime rate. Nannies should keep a weekly time sheet and submit this to the parent at the end of each pay period showing all hours worked. The nanny should sign the time sheet indicating she has received payment according to the hourly rate and hours worked.

Note: Parents that need an expectable 50-plus hours per week of childcare often come to an agreement with their nanny to pay an hourly rate for all hours worked and then "back into" the rate to show a lower rate for regular hours and 1.5 times that rate for the overtime hours. This total matches the agreed-on hourly rate for all hours worked. Parents agree to compensate a minimum of this amount weekly. The benefit: a lower-overtime, more-affordable rate for the family and a guaranteed weekly compensation for the nanny. Parents are urged to consult with their tax accountant for advice on handling overtime.

A cautionary note on overtime: The Domestic Worker's Rights Initiative is very active in advising nannies of their right to overtime, as well as other employment laws. Parents are urged to be attentive to these laws to ensure compliance.

Note: Parents should check with state and local employment laws to ensure compliance with these laws. Generally, laws that favor employees hold precedent. For example, California employment laws requires overtime to be paid for all hours over nine per day and 45 per week. The federal overtime law of over 40 hours per week overrides California State overtime law. In California, therefore, nannies are to be paid overtime for all hours worked over nine per day and 40 per week.

Hourly Rate

According to the 2014 International Nanny Association Survey[28], the average hourly rate nannies earn across the U.S. is $18.66, with higher rates paid to nannies with a college degree and/or more than five years' experience. This average is higher in certain cities, including those in the San Francisco Bay Area, where rates range from $20 to more than $30 per hour depending on the number of children cared for, years of experience and level of education.

---

28   http://www.nanny.org/wp-content/uploads/2015/03/2014_INA_Salary_Survey.pdf

LISA'S STORY

Lisa always bought at the top end of the market. She believed that the more you pay, the better you get. While she liked a good deal, she knew bargaining took time, and in her experience there was more risk involved with the end product. She didn't want to bargain with a nanny over salary. She didn't want the potential risk that the nanny would feel resentful and leave for a better-paying position. She also wanted the best she could afford. When she asked other moms about what they were paying their nannies, she found salaries ranged from $16 to $25 per hour. Some of the nannies earning at the low end of this range seemed competent and the parents satisfied with their work. Lisa wondered: is compensation an indicator of quality in the nanny market?

Benefits

The standard benefit package includes the following for full-time employment prorated for part-time status.

Vacation

Two weeks per year, accrued monthly.

Note: Parents can request that their nanny take 50 percent of her vacation weeks at the same time the family takes their vacation. This helps the parents, since they don't need to find a replacement when their nanny is on vacation while also paying their nanny's salary as an earned benefit.

A word to the wise

Budget 52 weeks of your nanny's salary! Parents should guarantee that their nanny will receive a weekly salary based on the expectable number of hours worked throughout the course of employment. This means that if you go away on vacation and your nanny does not take vacation or go with you, she receives her regular weekly salary. As her employer, however, you can expect that your nanny does work in lieu of childcare. This includes work related to childcare, such as organizing clothes, moving seasonal clothing into storage, organizing toys and play spaces and planning for activities for the coming months. Nannies leave families who dock their pay when the family is away. Better to treat your nanny as an employee with a guaranteed 52-week paycheck than to risk losing her and incur the time, cost and energy of finding a replacement.

Holidays

Seven holidays annually (Christmas, New Year's Day, Memorial Day, Independence Day, Labor Day, Thanksgiving and the day after Thanksgiving). If a holiday falls on a weekend, a nanny is given either the Friday or the Monday off during the week in which that holiday falls. For part-time employment a nanny is paid for a holiday she is scheduled to work.

Sick Leave Pay or Paid Time Off (PTO)

2015 federal laws require employers with fewer than 10 employees to provide one hour of paid sick leave for every 30 hours an employee works, with a cap of 40 hours of accrued leave per year. Employees begin to accrue sick leave after 90 days of work. Domestic employees, such as nannies, are covered under the law.

Nannies may use paid leave for their own medical needs or to care for family members, including registered domestic partners. Nannies with no spouse or partner may use the leave to care for a "designated person" such as a roommate or a neighbor.

Automobile

Parents provide a "nanny car" to drive their child or the nanny uses her own car.

If there is no nanny car available, parents may require their nanny to use her own car. Parents provide a nontaxable stipend based on government rates per mile to reimburse for gas and wear-and-tear. The amount of the stipend is determined based on estimated usage and is typically issued monthly.

Note: Parents as employer are vicariously liable to cover the cost of any accident or injury the nanny experiences while working for them. This can include a "fender-bender" in the grocery store parking lot or a personal injury accident. If a nanny uses the family car, she should be added as a second driver on the parent's automobile insurance policy. If a nanny uses her own car for work, parents are strongly advised to consult with their automobile agent or attorney for information on how to reduce vicarious liability.

Meals

Parents provide adequate and appropriate food for their nanny.

Parents are not responsible for providing meals for their live-out nanny. However, most families allow their nanny to take whatever food or drink she may want from the family's supplies, within reason. Parents often include on their grocery list special nanny requests to have around the house.

Room and Board

For live-in nannies.

Parents keep a stock of food supplies in the home for their nanny. Special requests for items the family typically doesn't use, within reason, are part of the regular shopping list.

Parents often provide some means of storing and preparing food in the nanny's living space, if possible. This can be as simple as a coffeemaker, electric kettle, microwave and mini-refrigerator. Nannies then have some privacy and opportunity to prepare simple meals away from the family's kitchen/dining area when they're not working.

Telephone

Use of the landline in the house for local calls or a cell phone for work-related calls only.

The nanny is responsible for the cost of all personal long-distance and unreasonably long toll calls from these telephones. Parents deduct this cost from her salary.

Nannies typically use their own cell phone for work and cover the expense within reason. If the parents require more than reasonable messaging or phone calls, a stipend is provided to cover this expense. Some parents provide the nanny with a cell phone for use during work.

Travel

Reimbursement of any necessary travel-related expenses, such as airfare, hotel, ground transportation and meals during any travel undertaken at the parents' request. Other important details follow:

- Nannies are not reimbursed for any non-travel-related, nonessential and/or personal expenses while traveling.

- Nannies receive their guaranteed pay plus compensation for any additional hours worked.

- Nannies work a flexible schedule during travel, to include evenings and weekends.

- If the child shares the same room as the nanny, she is paid for all hours worked. Parents pay the regular hourly rate until 10 p.m. and resume this hourly rate of pay at 6 a.m. Nannies can be paid a lower, "on-call" minimum hourly rate during sleep time. If the child wakes during the night, the Nanny is considered working and paid at her regular hourly rate. *Note:* Overtime rules apply.

- Some parents provide a bonus when a nanny travels with them, particularly for extended and difficult travel schedules.

Nonstandard benefits include the following:

Medical/Dental Insurance

Parents pay a nontaxable stipend to cover all or part of the monthly premiums on any policy held by their nanny. The nanny is responsible for any deductibles and co-payments.

- Monthly premiums can average between $90 and $600 per month. The cost of monthly premiums is based on a number of factors, including amount/type of coverage, deductible, age and/or geographic region.

- Parents either set up a payroll account to deduct the medical contribution from gross earnings or issue a check directly to their nanny made payable either to the insurance company or the nanny, with a notation it is for insurance reimbursement. This arrangement ensures monthly premiums are covered and provides a record of payment in the event of an audit.

Retirement

Parents issue a nontaxable stipend as a contribution to an Individual Retirement Account (IRA) held by the nanny. IRAs can be funded up to $5,500 per year ($6,500 per year over 50 years old).

- Parents either set up a payroll account to deduct the IRA contribution from gross earnings or issue a check directly to their nanny made payable to the IRA manager or to the nanny, with a notation it is for

IRA contribution. This arrangement ensures monthly contributions are covered and provides a record of payment in the event of an audit.

Continuing Education and Training

Parents provide an annual stipend to cover the cost of workshops, training and/or conferences related to child development, including reimbursement for any and all related costs, including airfare, hotel, ground transportation and meals.

- Nannies receive a guaranteed weekly salary if the training occurs during the week or are paid an hourly rate for training hours if training occurs on their days off.

Conditions of Employment

There are several very important conditions that a nanny candidate must meet.

- She will need to authorize you to process a check of her Social Security number (SSN) to ensure her identity. SSN verification gives the address and name history associated with the use of the SSN. This informs where and under what name(s) the criminal checks should be made. The SSN can be cross checked with an applicant's verbal and written work/personal history for inaccuracies or missing information.

- A criminal background check is standard for people working in childcare to ensure they have no prior criminal record. The most reliable is a criminal check in each county the candidate has resided in, using the name and verified social security number provided.

(In California, the TrustLine Registry[29] provides a state-wide check of three different indices using a candidate's fingerprints and photo identification: the California Department of Justice records, for any allegation or criminal convictions; the California Child Abuse Index, for any substantial allegations of child abuse and neglect; and a Federal Bureau of Investigations check, for federal crimes and misdemeanors. Candidates who have previously cleared with TrustLine can produce a clearance letter from TrustLine. Background checks can only be run with a candidate's written authorization. These forms are provided by the background check agency running the report.)

- Regardless of whether your nanny will drive while working for you, you'll want to gain access to her driving record to ensure she has no major accidents or excessive speeding tickets or other moving violations on her record. Repeated citations for speeding or numerous parking tickets can indicate impulsivity and/or irresponsibility. A driving-under-the-influence (DUI) citation can indicate alcohol or substance abuse.

- Verify that she is currently certified in CPR and has taken a First Aid training course, or ensure that she is willing to undergo the training as a condition of her employment if she has not yet had it, and is willing to recertify annually.

- TB testing. Tuberculosis is a bacterial infection spread through inhaling tiny droplets from the coughs or sneezes of an infected person. You'll want to ensure your nanny has a clear TB test. TB can be deadly for children under age four; thus, it's vital that your nanny be tested within the last year to ensure she is not a carrier, and retested annually as a condition of employment. Though rare, it's possible for adults to test positive for TB even if they have no

---

29   TrustLine Registry. https://www.trustline.org

symptoms. *Note:* Some non-U.S.-born nannies have been vaccinated against the disease during childhood and will test positive. In these situations, nannies must rule out being a carrier by getting a chest X-ray.

- Measles, Mumps and Rubella Vaccination (MMR): Some states require persons working in childcare settings to immunize against MMR. Please check with your State Public Health Department for vaccine requirements.

- Tetanus, Diphtheria, and Pertussis (Whooping Cough) Vaccination (TDaP): The TDaP vaccine gives protection from these serious diseases. Babies are considered vulnerable until six months to one year of age. All adults, including nannies, should be vaccinated. Parents of infants should consult with their pediatrician for recommendations.

In 1983 Mary Beth Phillips, a 30-year old mother of a 6-month old daughter returned home from her graduate class to find out that her daughter had been rushed to a hospital comatose and convulsing - a victim of violent shaking by her nanny. Three years later, the nanny was convicted of felony child abuse, fined $100, required to perform 2,000 hours of community service and put on five years' probation. Amazingly, the judge allowed the nanny to continue caring for children to support herself - with no way for parents to know what this nanny had done. The judge ignored pleas from Phillips and prosecuting attorneys from barring the nanny from working with children again. Angry and driven, Phillips started a campaign in Sacramento to spare other parents the horrible pain she had experienced. In 1993, the TrustLine Registry was formed.

A Word to the Wise: Not all Criminal Records Checks are Created Equal

By Lynn Peterson, Vice President of PFC Information Services, Inc.

There is a type of online criminal check that is purported to be a "nationwide" criminal check. This check goes by many names: the National Criminal Check, the Multi- State Criminal Check, the Multi- Jurisdictional Criminal Check, and the Nationwide County and State Criminal Check. Regardless of the label, these searches include the same data, which is robotically extracted through "screen scraping." Vendors claim that as many as 550 million criminal records are included. While those numbers sound impressive, anyone that utilizes this database search should read the fine print.

The Non-Existent Nationwide Criminal Check

While the National Criminal Check search sounds extremely good, because it contains millions of records, it is instant, and is very inexpensive; the reality is that there is no such thing as a true nationwide criminal check. For example, in the state of New York the only records included are sex offender and prison release records. The single legitimate way to check for criminal records statewide in New York is to search the New York Administrative Office of the Courts' felony and misdemeanor records. The reason that the "National" criminal database does not include data from this source is that New York charges $68.00 for this check. The "National" check relies solely on free records, which very often contain no identifying information, such as date of birth or Social Security number. Therefore, data is not only missing, it includes records that have absolutely nothing to do with your applicant. The results include both false positives and false negatives.

The Bottom Line

The "National" check is geographically wide, but is riddled with holes and inaccuracies. However, when targeted records checks are conducted using quality data, and identifying information in the locations where the individual has lived, the result is the most comprehensive criminal records search possible.

Documentation

The Department of Homeland Security requires parents to hire only those persons with documentation to work legally in the U.S. Parents are expected to check certain documents, make note of these on Form I-9, then sign and keep this form with their nanny's employment documents.

Because this market is unlicensed and unregulated, many nannies do not have documentation. It is important that you make decisions about documentation before you start. This decision affects the pool of available applicants, the advertising and prescreening for the position and the compensation arrangements you make with your nanny.

Experience

You'll need to determine the amount of and type of experience with children that you expect of your nanny and evaluate her track record. You should expect to see overall steady employment with families in a nanny's work history. In this field, two and a half years with a family can be considered "steady" employment. Many parents put their child in a preschool setting at two and a half or three years of age and let their nanny go at that time.

EVALUATION OF NEED: QUALITIES AND CHARACTERISTICS OF YOUR IDEAL NANNY

SARAH'S STORY

Sarah knew it was time to hire a mother's helper, but she was reluctant about starting the search. Since she had her daughter Violet almost two years ago, she'd put her career on hold. It was only recently that she started dabbling in freelance design work, but only during Violet's nap time or when her husband watched Violet on the weekends. Sarah loved being a stay-at-home mom, and the daily routine of reading, singing and playing with her daughter gave her immense joy. But it was also true that she missed her creative career and had a hankering to jump back in with her own freelance design business. She knew that to get a successful business up and running would take more than the few hours a week she had free while Violet was asleep. She'd need time to create, not to mention time to manage the logistics involved in running her own business. She resolved to talk with her husband about hiring a mother's helper, even though she had no idea what type of person she was looking for.

Evaluating what your childcare needs are includes more than choosing the days you want your nanny to work and determining how much you can afford to pay her (although these are important points). Discipline styles, religion, values, temperament and even seemingly innocuous points such as grooming are all issues you may want to consider as you decide what it truly is you need and want from your new nanny. In short, you want a nanny that clicks with your family.

When parents meet their right nanny for the first time, they often describe the experience as having a certain positive gut feeling or the right chemistry with her. Somehow the nanny seems right. It's the "aha" moment they've waited for! When a nanny doesn't feel right, they often attribute it to a lack of chemistry with the person. Somehow, they just didn't click.

In my work, I have found that the right fit between parents and nannies is an indicator of quality. The right fit increases the likelihood a nanny will develop a meaningful relationship with a child in partnership with the child's parents. The right fit also increases the likelihood that a nanny will continue providing childcare for as long as needed.

Both outcomes not only support a child's development of trust and competency but also minimize stress for parents. A child learns over time that a responsible adult will understand who he is and what he needs and respond in a predictable way. The parents can focus on parenting in partnership with someone they trust instead of going through the time-consuming and disruptive process of finding another nanny.

So how do you come up with this magical formula to calculate what you want and need in a nanny?

Talk with your spouse or partner about how you were raised. What was a typical day and how were the daily routines managed? How did your parents respond when you behaved counter to their expectations?

What was a particular saying about life your parents used that you would pass along to your child? What aspects of how they parented do you want to use, and what do you want to do differently?

The Character and Temperament of Your Ideal Nanny

There are other qualities you want to consider besides values, orientations and caregiving style. These are characteristics observable from appearance and those qualities you discern from her behavior.

Here are some areas you may want to consider when evaluating fit:

Age

Does chronological age matter? Consider this in terms of activity level, stamina and maturity. Will she have to carry your baby up and down stairs on a regular basis or run after an active toddler? Does she have enough life experience to assure you she can manage the challenges she will encounter? Is her personal life stable enough to ensure predictable employment with you for as long as you need her?

Grooming

Is the way she dresses consistent with how you want your family to be seen by others? Is there a certain dress code that is important for you?

Language

Can you understand each other well? Can you talk easily about the hows and whys of your child's day?

Temperament

Is she active and outgoing? Quiet? Formal with close boundaries or a "wear her heart on her sleeve" type? Does her temperament complement or run counter to yours? What about your child's?

Communication

Does her style of communicating mesh with yours or is it difficult to understand her ideas or to follow her line of thought?

BRIGITTE'S STORY

A Story About Mitigating—and Tolerating—Your Differences

Brigitte was a natural in the realm of the creative. She could turn a brown cardboard box into a castle that any princess would die for! Rosie and Brigitte would play for hours in the midst of glue, markers, stickers, ribbon, paper and sparkles. They would tell stories about the princess and the prince who would live there, how they met, the king and queen, and on and on. In the midst of this fantasy world, Brigitte would always forget about the time. Who would want to leave such a fantastical world and join those living in the here and now? So inevitably Jessica would come home to a very happy, excited little girl, a nanny who would readily recreate the fantasy world for Jessica to join—and a playroom full of glue, paper, markers and scissors! Oh, and not to overlook the lunch dishes still in the sink, unfolded laundry in the basket and half-eaten snacks everywhere. Brigitte was not the neatest person on the block or someone who cleaned up as she went. She was the type of person who would leave things undone until the end of the day and scurry around and clean up everything all at once—ideally if she stopped the play to get it done in time.

Well, this part of Brigitte's character really annoyed Jessica. She couldn't tolerate the mess at home. All day at work she dealt with chaos and put out fires. She really needed to come home to some order, peace and quiet! At the same time, she loved that Rosie had such joyful, creative days with Brigitte. But the bind she was in was real.

She told Brigitte, "I love that you're so creative and I love that Rosie is so happy with you and learning so much. But coming home to a house full of glue, paper, markers and scissors everywhere drives me crazy! The lunch dishes in the sink and half-eaten snacks here, there and everywhere is really over the top. Where I work, it's hectic all day; I'm busy putting out fires and it seems nothing ever gets done. When I come home, I need some order. Is there any way we could get the place straightened up before I get home?"

Brigitte admitted that time always got away from her. She wanted to get the place ready on time, and Rosie was at an age when it was right to learn about clean-up time. She suggested that Jessica text when 30 minutes away from home so she and Rosie could stop playing and have time to get the house in order.

This worked most days, but the reality was that Brigitte was not the most meticulous nanny and inevitably Jessica would find dishes left out and a bag of carrots in the playroom near the cardboard castle— and a little girl who would say, "Uh-oh! We missed that one!"

THE JOB DESCRIPTION

Precisely evaluating your childcare needs is half the battle of finding the right nanny for your family. You need to determine the working arrangements and the type of care you're looking for, as well as the basics like the days and hours you want your nanny to work, how much you can afford to pay her and what kinds of benefits you'll offer.

It's vital that you take the time to determine exactly what you want, need and can afford to offer before you begin working on a job description. Refer to Chapter 6 for specifics on job titles and responsibilities, as well as Chapter 7 for information on the nuts and bolts of hiring a nanny. Once you've made decisions about specifics like the type of nanny you need and the schedule that works best for you, use this checklist to complete the profile of what you're looking for in a nanny. A Job Description checklist follows to ensure you cover all the important details of your search. It is also included in the end of the book and/or you can download it on The Institute for Families and Nannies website: https://www.tiffan.org

Job Basics

Job Title	Nanny Arrangement	Documentations
Nanny	Live Out	Department of Homeland Security
Mother's Helper	Live-In	Internal Revenue Service
Family Assistant	Share Care	DMV (driver's license/ID)
Au-Pair	Co-op	Workers Compensation
Doula	Staffed Household	
Housecleaner		
Babysitter	**Schedule**	**Compensation**
Special Needs Therapist	Full Time	Salary Range_____ Wk/Mo/Yr
Tutor	Part Time	Taxable Income
	Flexible Hours/Days	
	Overnight Care	**Benefits**
		Travel
		Vacation
		Holidays
		Sick Pay
		Medical Insurance Premiums
		Retirement IRA Contribution
		Room and Board
		Cell Phone
		Nanny Car for personal use

Responsibilities

Childcare	Housework	Errands
Feeding	Child's room kept clean	Grocery shopping, as needed
Changing	Toys clean and put away	Dry cleaning
Bathing	Bed linens clean/put away	Post Office or FedEx/UPS
Providing Safe Care	Child's laundry	
Plan daily activities	Family laundry	**Pet Care**
Maintains daily journal	Family meal preparation	Feeding pet(s)
Child meal preparation	Cleans up after herself	
Tutoring	Straightens up main areas	
Transporting child		
Collaboration with professionals		

Requirements:

Education/Training	Childcare Experience	Languages
Early Childhood Education	Infant/toddler	English
State teaching credential	Preschool	Spanish
Special needs certification	Elementary	French
Continued education	Adolescent	German
Workshops	Group care	Chinese-Mandarin
	Multiples	Chinese-Cantonese
	Other	Other
Health Safety Requirements	**Background Check**	
CPR/First Aid training	Criminal in all counties resided	
TB test clearance	Social Security verification	
TiDaP and MMR vaccination	Driving record	
Flu shot	Civil Protective orders	

Employer-Employment Documents:

Employee Requirements	Employer Requirements	
Resume	Worker's Compensation	
References	Auto insurance for nanny	
Photo	Authorization to drive form	
Certificates of education/training	Emergency medical treatment form	
CPR/first aid certificate	Important phone numbers	
TB test clearance	Disaster plan	
Driving license		
Driving record		
Criminal and civil background check		
Social security verification		
IRS W-4		
DHS I-9		
Contract		

ADVERTISING: GETTING THE WORD OUT

To find the best pool of nanny candidates, you need to spread the word about what you're looking for. Post notices online, in mothers' group newsletters and on neighborhood bulletin boards. Ask relatives, friends and colleagues for leads. Investigate opportunities at community colleges and universities. Research online for prospective candidates.

If you've taken the time to create a job description, announcing the position is easy! You have made decisions about the basic yet most important criteria that should be posted.

Where possible, creatively use your job description to attract attention to the right candidates without narrowing the pool. If there is a particular characteristic that sets your position apart from others, make that a central part of the announcement. For example, wonderful children and casual family style, an above-market compensation package, lots of travel to exotic destinations or a desirable work schedule—these are all job specifics that might appeal to a particular type of nanny. You may also focus on the type of candidate you prefer, such as a graduate student or someone with fluency in a particular language.

There are few legal requirements governing what information you can include in your announcement. Unless you hire 15 or more employees, you are not required to comply with Title VII of the Civil Rights Act of

1964. Most websites and bulletin boards, however, do put limits on the amount and kind of information you can post. Most often they disallow content that degrades or is hateful toward individuals or groups.

Three Key Areas for Recruiting a Nanny

Word of mouth: Ask everyone you know if they know of a nanny seeking work. Parents know how hard it can be to find a great nanny and are often eager to help others.

Online bulletin boards: Most parents use online bulletin boards to recruit a nanny, and nannies consult them to find employment.

Local mothers' groups: Most local mothers' groups publish a monthly newsletter or newsgroup and share resources on nannies looking for work.

Remember the story I shared in the introduction about helping my friend find a nanny? I learned the hard way that you often need many candidates in order to get down to a short list of people you want to interview. Don't be afraid to cast a wide net and gather lots of possibilities. If you've worked through your criteria, winnowing the list down will be straightforward.

A sample Nanny Job Announcement is included in the end of the book and/or you can download it on The Institute for Families and Nannies website: https://www.tiffan.org

PRESCREENING

Evaluate prospective candidates over a phone call and email discussions to determine suitability. Many nanny candidates have created portfolios complete with résumé, letters of recommendation, certificates of education and background check clearances. These can be emailed for quick review. Check references on those candidates you are interested in interviewing. Select those candidates for interviews that meet basic requirements and have at least two or three of the "must have" qualities from your evaluation checklist.

Following are some prescreening guidelines for separating the fit from the not so fit.

1. Describe your nanny position requirements, such as schedule, start date, responsibilities, age of your child and other expectations such as documentation, taxable income, car, etc.

2. If she is interested and can meet the expectations, ask questions to learn what her experience has been with children.

3. If you are interested based on her response and your impression of how easily you can communicate with her, ask for three references you can check.

4. Advise her of the other conditions of employment: authorization to process a check of her Social Security number, criminal and driving records; CPR/First Aid training; and TB testing.

5. Advise her you will contact her within 24 hours to schedule an interview if you are interested. Find out if she is in serious discussions with a potential employer, and proceed to meet sooner if needed.

When recruiting and screening candidates, it can be very helpful and meaningful to understand a candidate's personal history. This information can provide insight into a candidate's closely held values and child-rearing orientations, informing how closely aligned they are to yours. However, parents should be cautious when entering this line of questioning. Title VII of the Civil Rights Act of 1964 forbids employers to ask questions related to race, color, religion, sex and national origin.[30] While strictly speaking this law does not apply to those with fewer than 15 employees, professional organizations recommend that parents follow these guidelines.

To eliminate these concerns, parents should consider questions that relate to skills, values and use of judgment. As an example, "What are the three values that you believe are important for children to learn about the world? How do you teach these?"

Sample Screening Questions are included in the end of the book and/ or you can download them on The Institute for Families and Nannies website: https://www.tiffan.org

---

30   Title VII of the Civil Rights Act of 1964. https://www.eeoc.gov/laws/statutes/titlevii.cfm

CHECKING REFERENCES

Don't be tempted to skip this step in the process, even if you know the nanny or she comes highly recommended. As I've said previously, just because a nanny is a fit for another family doesn't mean she is right for you. Checking references is an opportunity for you to gather lots of information about the nanny, including her personality, experience and how she works, so that you can determine whether she's a candidate you want to interview.

Meaningful Questions and Key Concerns

Most parents are concerned about whether a reference is a legitimate one and what questions can be asked of references to get a good understanding of the applicant's character, skill and style with children. It has been my experience that nanny candidates rarely pass along a false reference. Parents should assume a reference is legitimate and should ask thoughtful questions. A good reference will be able to answer questions that relate to the candidate's interactions with her child. The reference's comments should be positive but balanced, with some areas of recommendation relatively stronger than others. Most references can cite areas where a candidate can use improvement. In all cases, references should be able to back up their comments with examples.

Assumptions About References

1. References want to do right by the person who has cared for their children and give a positive recommendation.

2. References prefer not to give a negative recommendation to minimize any potential conflicts with their previous nanny.

3. A reference's experience with a nanny may not be the same as what you will experience with the nanny.

4. References should have an opinion about both the positive and negative characteristics of a nanny and provide suggestions about areas in which a nanny could improve. Parents who have fired a nanny for a breach of trust, neglect of their child or recurring incidents of irresponsibility are almost always honest and forthright about their experience. They may provide this information on the condition it is kept confidential.

Whether a comment is positive or negative, ask for an example, and probe more if the comment would impact your decision to hire the applicant. For example, "She said open communication is really important for her, and at the same time she's had several jobs that ended after a short period of time. How did communication work with you and her?"

Meaningful Questions to Ask References

1. Verify dates of employment ages of children, responsibilities and reason for termination.

2. Was the nanny reliable and responsible in carrying out her duties (e.g., on time, seldom sick, flexible to stay later or work different hours)?

3. What was a typical day with the children?

4. What did the children like or not like about her?

5. How adept was she at meeting the developmental needs of their child and family as the children and family grew through one stage and into another?

6. Would they characterize her as honest and trustworthy?

7. What did the parents like or not like about her?

8. What would they want to see her do differently?

It is always best to get examples from references who are able to provide supporting evidence for what they say. If the kids were happy to see their nanny, what was it about her that made them so happy, and can they give an example of this?

Key Concerns: Alcohol/Substance Abuse, Child Abuse and Neglect

Before ending your conversation with a reference, you may consider asking the following questions to rule out potential abuse. You can preface it with, "I would like to ask you these last three questions that have nothing to do with what you have told me about your nanny. As you can imagine, she is a stranger to me and I am asking her to care for the most important people in my life."

1. Were there any indications of alcohol or substance abuse?

2. Is there anything in the way she responded to the children that would cause you concern, such as being overly harsh or critical, or punishing, hitting, hurting or otherwise harming your child?

3. Is there anything in her personal history that would indicate any criminal activity or allegations of criminal history?

You should hear an unequivocal no to each of the above questions.

Sample Reference Questions are included in the end of the book and/or you can download it on The Institute for Families and Nannies website: https://www.tiffan.org

THE INTERVIEW PROCESS

Face-to-face interviews are perhaps the most critical part of the nanny search process. You'll have the opportunity to look your candidates in the eye, hear how they answer your questions and draw your own conclusions about their suitability for your family. Invest the time needed to prepare for these meetings and don't skimp on the time required to conduct thorough interviews. You'll make a better hire and potentially save yourself the time and aggravation of having to hire a new nanny after making a hasty decision.

Note: Some parents prefer to start the interview process as a "speed-dating" event. They schedule candidates back-to-back for thirty minutes each to meet and greet and get an initial impression of the candidate. In my experience, this format works best with families that have hired nannies before or have gone through a round of more extensive interviews with three or four nannies. They know what they want. Time is limited. They are quick decision-makers. They prefer to see more candidates than fewer to get a broad view of the current market. They have done a reasonable screening to meet only those who match basic requirements. They never hire after a speed-dating event. Second interviews to confirm initial impressions always follow.

The standard protocol is to conduct a formal first interview with three to five good candidates, followed by an informal second interview with one or two finalists. Trial periods with one, potentially two, candidates complete the decision process. Along the way, evaluate for fit using the criteria you've developed. Use your gut to support what you see on paper and what references have said about the candidate. Remember: you have to like the person you are hiring as much as respect the work she has done with other families.

Evaluating and Eliminating Candidates

If I can give one important piece of advice about interviewing nanny candidates, it is this: Never hire someone after the first meeting. This is too important a decision to make based on "love at first sight"! Many of us have met someone on a first date, felt certain the person was the "perfect one" and then, after a second meeting, wondered what the brief love affair was about. Meeting nannies can be similar. For such an important decision, meeting more than once before hiring simply makes good sense.

The First Interview

The first interview is somewhat formal. This is a time to clarify the terms of the position, as well as get to know the candidate, both in terms of her childcare experience and her personal character.

Ideally, schedule two candidates back-to-back for an hour each with a fifteen-minute break between them. Schedule four or five candidates within a week's period. Scheduling in this way makes good use of your time and allows you to meet candidates close enough together in time that they are fresh in your mind. Evaluating one against another is easier. Doing interviews this way also prevents losing good candidates to another family because you waited too long to bring them back.

Topics to Cover

1. Position requirements: schedule, responsibilities, preferred start date and other particulars and/or idiosyncrasies of your position

2. Candidate's childcare experience

3. Candidate's character and style

4. Candidate's child-rearing philosophies and orientations

It is unrealistic to expect you will learn everything you need to know about a candidate in the first interview. At the same time, you should address each of these areas while also inviting the candidate to ask similar questions about your family and the position. Your goal in the first interview is twofold: to get answers to essential questions and to evaluate how easily you can communicate about these issues with her. In these discussions, you want to look for similarities in her responses and how you might respond. Remember: the purpose of the questions is not to get a "correct" answer! You want to learn about the amount of experience the candidate has had in those areas she will likely encounter, the range of skills she has developed when navigating these, her use of judgment and her capacity to discuss these issues with you. Rather than looking for "correct" answers, consider how easy it is to have a discussion with her about the area you are questioning. Look for breadth of knowledge compared with a specific answer. Consider how you might work together figuring out how to solve a problem.

Most parents experience a certain gut reaction to a candidate during the first interview. It is important to try to put words to this reaction. This will help as you evaluate the different candidates you meet.

For example, you may meet a candidate at the door and get an immediate, strong negative reaction. Perhaps she reminds you of someone you don't like or has a style or appearance that is less than desirable. Maybe she seems too rough around the edges or too loud and chatty or too quiet and unassuming. As a rule of thumb, I find it best to stay the course. Don't show her the door by ending the interview in 15 minutes. Take a deep breath. Pay attention to your immediate reaction and give both the candidate and yourself the opportunity to go through the interview. Then evaluate whether your initial reaction is either confirmed or changed. It's also worth acknowledging that interviewing is stressful for nannies, and this can influence how they first present themselves. Some nannies are slow to warm up and can initially seem shy or hesitant. Some attempt to manage their anxiety by talking too much. Some minimize their knowledge or experience in deference to their potential employers.

Cultural differences can affect the interview process. For example, a discussion about money in a first meeting is often "off the table" for parents in America. When a non-U.S.-born nanny asks in the first interview, "How much do you pay?", most parents have an immediate response that the nanny is intrusive, not sophisticated and more interested in money than in their child. By contrast, the nanny may believe she is being professional by raising an important issue directly.

Socioeconomic differences can also enter the interview process. Many nannies who provide excellent childcare came into the profession without the need for the formalities required by other professions. The use of portfolios with résumés, letters of recommendation and certificates of education and the protocols of how to interview successfully were neither needed nor taught. Many nannies found work through word of mouth. Although the nanny industry is becoming more professionalized, many nannies haven't developed the skills to present their work professionally. It can be disconcerting and frustrating for parents to go through the search process with a candidate pool that can be largely informal and nonprofessional when it comes to presenting their work histories and having polished interviewing skills.

Next Steps

After the initial round of interviews with candidates, most parents select one or two finalists and proceed to a second interview with them. Send rejected candidates a note of appreciation for their time and interest.

Note: Some parents interview five or more candidates and find that none meets their expectations. If this happens, you may consider the following:

1. Evaluate your job announcement and prescreening of candidates. You may be attracting candidates who don't meet your expectations.

2. Evaluate your job expectations and ideal nanny criteria. They may be unrealistic, or so specific as to narrow the pool of available candidates to a point where you are looking for a needle in the haystack. At times, it can be useful to get an objective opinion from close friends.

3. Pay closer attention to your feelings about hiring a nanny. Consider whether they interfere with your evaluation of candidates or your decision to hire anyone to care for your child. Some parents learn through the interview process that they don't want a nanny. They really want to stay home and be the sole provider of care. As mentioned earlier, this decision can be a positive outcome of the nanny search.

The Second Interview

The second interview is less formal and provides an opportunity for you to gather more information about the nanny and watch her in action with your child. Over the course of one to two hours, evaluate your candidate in the following ways:

1. Get to know the nanny better, particularly her character, temperament and communication style.

2. Ask questions in the areas you need to understand more.

3. Observe her in the direct care of the children.

4. Clarify and agree on the terms of your position: start date, responsibilities, compensation and benefits.

5. Review the conditions of employment: TB testing, CPR/First Aid training, TiDaP vaccination, clean driving record and criminal background check clearance.

Most parents get a positive confirmation after the second interview with a candidate and offer her the position based on the completion of a successful one-to-two-week trial period. In some situations, parents feel positive about a candidate but are hesitant to offer the position because of concerns in a particular area. Perhaps they worry whether the nanny has enough experience to discipline their active toddler, or the skills to keep infant twins on a similar daily routine. In these situations, it can be useful to let the candidate know what strengths influence your decision to hire her and which areas you have some questions about.

In most situations, the candidate's relative skills in these areas are better understood during the trial. If the decision is not to hire the candidate after the trial, it is easier on everyone if the concerns have been raised and discussed beforehand. Some parents decide to hire the candidate and provide support in areas where she may need it.

Sample Interview Questions are included in the end of the book and/or you can download it on The Institute for Families and Nannies website: https://www.tiffan.org

THE TRIAL PERIOD

Even if you're certain you've found your perfect nanny, it makes sense to have a trial period just to confirm what you believe to be true. It's helpful for both families and nannies to be sure the match is a good one before contracts are signed.

A trial period shows intent to hire. As such, it is scheduled and paid. It is nonbinding on both sides—an opportunity for everyone to know whether this is the right situation.

The trial period gives both parents and the nanny the opportunity to get to know each other better. It is also an opportunity for the nanny and child to begin their relationship with the support of the parents. The nanny receives training by the parent or the previous nanny in the care of the children, information on the regular household responsibilities and knowledge about the neighborhood and local community where activities will happen.

Many parents recognize but often place little value on the need for their child to trust their nanny before they look to her for help or comfort or take direction from her. This is particularly important for children who need time to warm up to others and/or for toddlers and preschool children who need to learn she is the person their parents trust to keep them safe. This is a time parents can help their nanny learn how they respond to the children when they act a certain way so the nanny, using her own style, can respond in ways similar enough that the children feel life is predictable. When evaluating your nanny, pay close attention to how well she listens, takes direction and recognizes differences among children, and the style she uses to implement what you both feel is important to care for and teach the children.

During the trial, parents are often closely attuned to how their children respond to their new nanny. If their child protests or doesn't warm up easily, they often attribute this to their nanny's lack of experience or inability to get in tune with their child. While this may be true, it can also be true that the child is responding negatively for other reasons. Some include protesting against having anyone other than his parent care for him, reluctance to respond favorably toward anyone until he feels the parents are confident he will be safe in their care, or responding to the loss of a previous nanny and wishing she would return.

Most often, the trial period is a time when both parents and nannies get confirmation that this is a good match and begin the honeymoon phase of their working relationship. Often the parents feel incredibly relieved to have found someone to care responsibly for their child, and the nanny feels incredibly relieved to have found a family she can be part of and employers who respect the work she does for them.

It is expected that at the end of the trial period, both parents and nanny are in agreement about working together, have agreed on the terms that are written in a contract and the nanny has either successfully completed the requirements for employment or is in the process of completing them.

CONTRACTS

Based on my work with hundreds of families, I am a strong proponent of contracts between nannies and families. The parent/nanny relationship often slips into the familiar territory of the nanny being "one of family" versus an employee being compensated for work performed. Contracts between parents and nannies make it clear who is the employer and who is the employee.

Conduct a formal closure meeting to review and confirm the procedures on how to handle medical/police/fire/disaster emergencies; review employment documents; and review and sign the contract.

There are three important reasons for using a written contract with your nanny:

1. It minimizes misunderstandings about expectations, particularly about compensation/benefits/schedule and house rules.

2. It balances the parent/nanny relationship by formalizing the employer/employee side of the relationship.

3. It provides a basis to evaluate performance over time.

Some parents do not want the formalities of a signed contract with their nanny. They can be concerned about locking themselves into a situation they can't get out of. Some worry their nanny might take them to court for an alleged breach of contract. Others are concerned they are more vulnerable to retribution by government agencies if they have a signed contract with an undocumented worker or with a nanny who gets paid under the table. While there are various opinions about whether these concerns have merit, the reasons for using a contract are compelling. There is ample opportunity for misunderstandings to occur in the parent-nanny relationship! Having a good discussion and formal agreement about what is expected on both sides can minimize them.

On the website for The Institute for Families and Nannies, you can download a sample nanny contract that you can modify to suit your particular situation. The contract is an at-will agreement that either party can terminate without cause. The terms describing conditions of termination, compensation/benefits, rules of the house and many other meaningful aspects of employment are outlined in the sample contract. I suggest you review the contract and the details of compensation/ benefits in Chapter 9: The Job Description to personalize your contract and better understand the terms of the sample contract. Parents draft the contract and send it to their nanny for review and comment. In most cases, the terms are acceptable, particularly if you have discussed them in the prescreening and interview phase.

A Sample Contract is included in the end of the book and/or you can download it on The Institute for Families and Nannies website: https://www.tiffan.org

BRITTANY'S STORY

The Win-Win Relationship

Rosanna was one of those nannies who always wanted to make sure everyone was happy. Her employers loved that about her. Rosanna was always in the background, humming along and getting things done. She was there when needed and would do whatever was required to please her employer.

But there were compromises. Communicating explicitly and directly was implicitly "off the table." When you asked Rosanna a question, instead of getting a specific answer you got something that was "off the mark." It would take a little creativity to get the answer, and it always felt like a drive around the block searching for the house you knew was there but couldn't quite find.

For Brittany, this implicit way of communicating worked. In fact, she was relieved to have a nanny who didn't require checklists, direction and lots boundaries and rules. Over the years, Brittany and Rosanna developed a working relationship implicitly based on the standard that they would do right by each other. Rosanna always looked for ways to accommodate and please. Brittany gave her lots of hours and good pay. This was a win-win for Rosanna and Brittany.

Under the surface, unacknowledged by both, lay a subtle exchange of power that went beyond the boundaries of their working relationship. Rosanna lived very modestly. Brittany lived very luxuriously. Every so often, Rosanna crossed the boundaries of employment relationships. She would ask Brittany for a loan to pay for a new car or to get the designer sofa instead of giving it to charity. Brittany never refused. She elevated these boundary transgressions to a higher moral ground. To her, meeting these requests was the right thing to do for an employee who needed money and was so loyal.

Slowly over time, however, these breaks in the boundaries began to wear on both of them. Brittany began to feel Rosanna was taking advantage of her generosity. She resented having the economic differences between them put her at a disadvantage. She felt hostage to socioeconomic disparities she didn't create. Rosanna began to feel Brittany was taking advantage of her loyalty and hard work. She felt trapped in a relationship she needed in order to manage her finances. Her early appreciation of Brittany's loans and gifts had transformed into "golden handcuffs." Pleasing her employer felt like entrapment.

So after six years, they mutually agreed it was time to move on. Brittany gave Rosanna a nice severance and strong recommendations. Rosanna gave Brittany "best nanny employer" status to her replacement. The tension between them was repaired in characteristic style and Rosanna went on to please another employer who needed her.

DADS AND NANNIES

Hello, dads! It's great to know you're reading this chapter because so far, you may have felt left out of this discussion, and that was not my intention.

When it comes to hiring and working with a nanny, the "third" in the family constellation, it is most common that the discussion focuses on the mother-child-nanny relationship. This emanates from the widely held notion, reinforced by volumes of articles, media, literature and research, that the mother-child relationship is the most complex and challenging dynamic when it comes to determining how children develop. When a nanny enters the family, we often turn full attention to how this affects the mother, her maternal identity and the developing relationship between her and the child.

So, what about dads?[31] If we acknowledge, rightfully so, that dads are significant stakeholders in hiring and keeping the family's nanny, why are they secondary or ignored altogether?

---

31   NOTE: In this discussion, the title and role of "dad" is not exclusive to the husband/ wife marital relationship. Dads include the "other" parent and can be a female or male, as in LGBT relationships. Dad can be the "imagined other" partner in single-parent households. Dads may or may not reside in the same household, as in separated/divorced parents. Dads can be the "other" partner in blended families or the stepparent.

Here's one reason: the media hasn't been so positive about dads and nannies. In fact, the media thrives on sensationalizing the lives of rich and famous dads having affairs with their nannies. Arnold Schwarzenegger, Robin Williams, Jude Law and Ben Affleck have given the media and the public plenty of material to discuss endlessly and attempt to unravel the mysteries of why dads are attracted to their nannies. The narrative seems to be that men are egocentric, narcissistic, neurotic, obsessed with power and therefore attracted to a submissive nanny, fueling a dad's desire to be loved, cared for and doted on. Subsequently, warnings go out to moms to analyze their partner for such weak tendencies and to ensure the requirement "non-attractive" is placed high on the nanny criteria list!

Nannies are also advised to be on the watch for roving dads "pawing, playing with and pining for the babysitter."[32] Nannies complain that this unspoken elephant in the room occurs often enough to make it expectable. When deciding which family is the right fit, novice nannies are warned to be mindful of a dad's flirtatious behavior. Nannies don't want to be seduced by their employer and/or constantly fending off unwanted advances.

Between general assumptions that dads are less important than mothers and media reports about dads seducing nannies, it's no wonder that many dads would choose to remain the silent "third"!

Dads as Decision-makers: Sharing the Responsibilities for Childcare Support

One of the major decisions that comes with the responsibility of raising a child and must be faced by both parents is about whether, what

---

32 http://www.nydailynews.com/archives/lifestyle/dad-bad-new-york-city-nannies-dish-flirting-fathers-living-article-1.633604

amount and what kind of childcare support is needed. Will both parents work? Will one parent be home for all or part of the time? Which parent? How will this decision affect the family budget? Will it involve changing the family lifestyle, housing and/or employment? Becoming a parent is a major life transition and, by default, dads are involved.[33]

When it comes to childcare decisions, dads may find themselves in a major dilemma. Social and cultural norms, despite huge advances over the past 50 years giving women options to continue working while raising their children, place the burden on the mother to make the decision of whether to work while raising a family. Dads can choose an extended paternity leave or elect to be a stay-at-home dad, but the numbers of dads choosing this option are low[34]. As a result, dads can find themselves neither in the driver's seat about the childcare decision nor in a 50-50 shared role about the decision. Almost by default, dads end up in the supportive role to the mother as she makes her decision about whether to work while raising a family. Does she want to work outside the home? If so, how much? What options does she have? What will be the effect on her career? How a dad provides support to the mother as she struggles with her decision, and the kind of support he provides, has an impact on the relationship the parents have with each other and with the caregiver.

When it comes to hiring a nanny, the dad's supportive role intensifies. The intimacy in the employment relationship between the mother and nanny can further sideline him into this secondary role. To ensure a successful integration of the nanny into the family constellation, dads often find themselves supporting the mother as she manages her feelings about hiring and sharing the parenting role with a nanny. How well dads provide this needed support, to a greater or lesser degree,

---

33 This does not exclude the reality that some dads abdicate their parenting responsibilities altogether.

34 http://www.pewsocialtrends.org/2014/06/05/growing-number-of-dads-home-with-the-kids/

impacts how the nanny search goes, whom they hire and how the nanny will impact the couple's relationship.

Dads as Decision-makers: The Nanny Search

Despite the dilemma dads face when they're "second banana" in the decision of whether to hire a nanny in the first place, once that decision is made, many dads feel comfortable diving right into the shared role of making pragmatic choices. This includes the nanny's schedule, compensation/benefits, legal issues, required experiences and skills and the ideal qualities and characteristics of the nanny. Many dads recognize there's a lot at stake when considering whom to hire and have much to contribute, readily sharing ideas and opinions. In my experience, this collaborative decision-making around the pragmatics of the search is rewarding and mutually satisfying. Finally, the childcare decision is clarified, the road map defined and both parties are fully on board!

At this point, divisions of labor between the couple tend to happen. The mother, most often because she is on maternity leave when the search begins, assumes most of the responsibility for managing the details of the process. The dad generally steps into the supportive role, assisting her as she navigates the pragmatics and the emotional landscape. Almost universally, dads participate in the decision about whom to hire. In my experience, however, dads often defer to the mother's feeling about the best nanny to hire. It is assumed that the quality of the relationship between the mother and nanny determines how well the care will go, how long the nanny will stay with the family and how satisfied both parents will be with the nanny and the care she provides to their child.

Different divisions of labor happen as well. For example, dads who begin paternity leave after their partner returns to work or those who choose to be stay-at-home dads assume the responsibility for managing the details and much of the decision-making around the search.

The Family Constellation: The Nanny's Impact on the Couple's Relationship

How a nanny will influence your relationship is idiosyncratic to you, your partner and the nanny you hire. It will also change over time. The important point is that integrating a nanny into the family constellation influences the couple's relationship in ways that are not always predictable or easily understood. Even delegating the management of the nanny to one parent causes an effect. This can be welcomed, as in feelings of satisfaction at creating a cohesive working relationship among all adults and observing the healthy growth of the child; or unexpected and stressful, as in situations where one parent feels burdened by managing constant upheavals in the nanny relationship and dissonance in the care of the child. Parents can feel pulled by the differences among adults in how to provide care or being left out of important decisions altogether. This form of splitting among adults can create havoc in the couple's relationship, ultimately giving the nanny more power in the childcare arrangement than otherwise would exist when couples present a more unified front.

MARK'S STORY

A Married Dad

Mark was a stand-up kind of guy. Among close friends, he was known to be tough on the outside and soft on the inside. He and Miranda were in their mid-30s and on the rise in their careers when they decided it was time to have a child. The decision came out of their heart-to-heart talks about parenting and sharing the responsibility for childcare. They didn't want to fall into traditional roles, with Miranda doing the bulk of childcare as a "second shift"[35] to working full-time. Mark would change diapers, clean bottles, feed, burp and take Dylan out for regular walks just like Miranda would. In the months after Dylan was born, Mark fell in love with him and felt fulfilled in a way he never had expected.

Mark also felt lucky in his relationship with Miranda. She was laid-back and somewhat secure as a new mom. She didn't hover around him making corrections or giving unrequested advice about how to care for Dylan. When Dylan was fussy on Mark's watch, she didn't rush in to "rescue" Dylan and do it "right."

Miranda took three months of maternity leave, followed by Mark's three months of paternity leave. During this time, they went through a successful process to hire Lisa as their nanny. Because Miranda returned to work when the process had started, they decided that Mark would be the go-to person to prescreen and schedule interviews with candidates. By default, he was the one to train Lisa during the trial period. Yet being the "go-to" parent didn't translate to being the decision-maker. He and Miranda interviewed and evaluated all the candidates together. Their decision to hire Lisa was mutual and based on experience, character and availability.

---

35   Arlie Hoschschild, *The Second Shift* (New York: Viking Penguin, 1989).

An interesting and unexpected blip in this otherwise mutual partnership came after Lisa started. It was, as some might say, a communication problem. When Lisa had a question about Dylan, she would bring it up to Miranda and they would make decisions together about how to handle it. Miranda would bring it up to Mark later. If Mark disagreed, Miranda would usually respond, "Interesting—let's see how it goes and we'll try that next time." But slowly over the months, the communication bond between Lisa and Miranda on Dylan's care cemented and Mark began to withdraw. It wasn't a conscious decision. It was more a subtle feeling of exclusion with a bit of resentment at having some of his "dad role" taken over by his nanny.

Miranda felt this also. It wasn't explicit, but came from Mark's singular responses to her comments about what she and Lisa had discussed about Dylan's latest challenge. Mark simply would say, "It looks like you both have it figured out."

Over a few beers one night with his best friend, Zachary, the subject came up about dads and nannies and moms. Zachary's experience with this triangular relationship was different. Their nanny had created something of a "good cop/bad cop" dynamic in their household. Zachary's wife, Susie, was formal and at times controlling in her relationship with their nanny. While there was a mutual respect between them, there was little warmth in their interactions. This mutual respect would shatter when Susie, under pressure at work, would turn and take out her frustrations on the nanny. Susie would then come to Zachary with a list of complaints and a mandate that it was about time to fire her. In turn, Zachary would come to the nanny's defense. He didn't want to go through an exhausting search only to recreate the wheel with a different nanny. In response, Susie would say, "I can never talk to you about this. You always take her side!"

Mark and Zachary were good friends and they were both decision-makers. They could see beyond their complaints and realize there was a bigger picture to figure out. Mark ordered another beer. He said, "You know, our experiences sound different, but in fact they're very similar. Somehow, we have slipped into a passive role in this complicated mother-dad-nanny relationship. We've assumed that because the mother-nanny-child relationship is most important and the most challenging, our role is to provide support when requested or when we realize it's needed. But for us, taking such a passive position has backfired. We end up putting Band-Aids on problems or feeling marginalized and resentful."

Zachary agreed—and it wasn't the beer that provided insight! It was Mark's point of reference that it takes "three to tango" and that there are no "bad guys" to blame for the position they found themselves in. Taking full charge of what they believed to be the source of the problem, they decided to create a more unified front with their partners vis-à-vis their nannies. They resolved to schedule weekly one-hour parent-nanny meetings to create a more stable working relationship around the care of their child. Weekly meetings could morph into biweekly or monthly meetings based on the outcome, but the important point was to take a more active role in the triadic relationship with their nanny.

Dad "Tips" for Managing the Nanny Relationship

1. Support the emotional landscape. Remember: neither you nor your partner are in complete control of the feelings you will have, when they will occur or how intensely you will feel them. When you or your partner become overwhelmed by the task at hand and act in ways that are not usual, set limits on the behavior but don't fault the person for having the feelings.

2. Acknowledge the challenges ahead. Don't underestimate how difficult it can be to manage the details of a search process and the decision about whom to hire. When problems arise, don't assume they could have been prevented. Even the most organized couples can be undone by the unexpected.

3. Make a mutually informed hiring decision. While you may defer to your partner about whom to hire, you should both acknowledge what was important to make it the right decision. If the decision turns out not to have been right, you have a basis on which to make a different one the next time around.

4. Work as a team. While it is a good idea to designate one partner as the "go-to" parent to manage the nanny relationship, any directions or decisions given to the nanny must be mutual. You simply don't want your nanny to "split" your relationship by going to you for what you will give her and to your partner for something else.

Dads Going Solo: Single Parenting

While still far more common among women, single parenting among men has become more prevalent in the past 20 years, primarily due to in-vitro fertilization but also to more flexible adoption policies giving single dads[36] an opportunity to parent without a partner. This life choice most often requires childcare support and for many single dads, hiring a nanny is the right form of care as it gives the most flexibility for solo parenting.

When it comes to hiring a nanny, single dads have a unique challenge. Unlike coupled parents, there isn't a "third," a mother present in the family constellation. Single dads should acknowledge that regardless of a their own social, religious or political beliefs, there are widespread cultural norms presuming that all children need both a mother and a father. Questions of "who is the mother" and/or "where is the mother" of this child can hover ghost-like around both dad and nanny.

This expectation may come up innocently in normal social interactions, such as when a nanny registers the child to take a "Mommy and Me" class at the library and is asked about the mother. Or a stranger admiring the baby at a local café may comment, "What a cute baby you have! She looks just like you!" Implicit in these interactions lies the expectation that this child has a mother who can be identified.

More subtle is the elephant in the space between a single dad and the nanny. If the nanny spends many hours of the day over the course of weeks, months and years caring for her "charge," then does nurture override nature? Can the nanny fill the role of mother, even in fantasy?

When single dads hire a nanny, this question of "Who is the mother?" can be addressed when evaluating candidates by asking "what if" questions during an interview. Here are a few to consider. There are no right or wrong answers here; of most importance is to voice potentially sensitive issues and set a foundation for future discussions if/when needed.

---

36   In addition to parents using IVF or adoption, single parenting includes men and women parenting solo due to death of a partner, separation or divorce.

You will be creating a relationship with my child, ideally one that is close and personal.

1. If a stranger asks you, "Are you the mother" what might you say?

2. If my son asked you, "Are you my mom?" what would you say?

3. If my child asked you, "Who is my mom?" what would you say?

Finally, it's tough going solo! Single dads may inadvertently lean heavily on their nanny for personal and emotional support. At times you may need a shoulder to cry on or advice about the new person you are dating. A word to the wise: don't put your nanny in the position to be your therapist, your mother or your advisor.

DANIEL'S STORY

A Single Dad

Daniel was a divorced and successful attorney in his 40s with no kids. His friends labeled him as SINK (Single Income No Kids) and a definite candidate for Bachelor of the Year! A real catch for any woman, there were many lining up at Daniel's door. But after 10 years of high-intensity romances, travel to exotic adventure destinations, fast-paced city living and accumulating wealth, a strange change began happening. Daniel began yearning for a child of his own. On his 40th birthday in 2012 with no "wife prospects" on the horizon, Daniel made the decision to hire a surrogate to carry his child and a live-in nanny to work long days and possibly well into the evenings to manage Daniel's hectic work schedule after paternity leave.

This process to fatherhood opened a world that both fascinated and challenged Daniel. True to character, as a man of action, charm and decisiveness and with recommendations from friends, he found the perfect surrogate and nanny for this arrangement.

Life was good, if a bit shaky. Nagging thoughts pressed inward, waking him at 3 a.m., leaving Daniel searching for answers to questions he hadn't expected. Does a child have the right to a mom? Who would be his baby's mom—the surrogate or nanny? What holds more weight—nature or nurture? Would the surrogate be the mom because of biology or the nanny because of nurture? Can a child have both or only one, or even none?

Daniel was a pragmatist and a man who directed his own life's journey. A surrogate is not "mom," and neither is a nanny. His son would create relationships with women who would at times take on the role of a nurturing mom or a soul-mate mom or a mom to fulfill what he needed at a certain time. Daniel also accepted the reality that his son might defy him later in life, insisting on his right to know who his mom is and to venture out singularly in the pursuit of finding her.

Despite Daniel's resolving the "who is mom" question, an uneasy conflict remained. If Daniel hired a nanny to live in his house and provide loving, responsible and consistent care for his son when he needed her, then it wasn't a major leap of faith to expect she would feel "like mom" and maybe act as though she is "the mom," particularly when there was no one around claiming this most highly esteemed role. Nothing in Daniel's strategic, direct and success-driven style of decision-making had prepared him to reconcile this conflict: hiring a warm, loving, knowledgeable and flexible nanny who would devote her life to caring for his child yet ensuring she would not, at times or always, feel and act like the mother of his child.

SAM'S STORY

A Divorced Dad

Sam and Kathy's marriage had been shaky from the start and deteriorated when their kids were born. The pressure in their work lives, managing the daily care of the kids, the kids' changing behavior and the household responsibilities pushed the limits beyond what they, as a married couple, could tolerate. After years of arguing, complaining, frustrations and attempts to make their relationship work better, they mutually decided to separate and filed for divorce. Sam moved into an apartment and Kathy stayed in the home. They shared equal custody of the children, rotating through the week and weekends to give them equal time with the kids.

What to do about Sonia, their beloved nanny who had been there through all the ups and downs of their marital relationship? It was clear she should continue, but should she work only for Kathy or for both? Sam and Kathy, in discussions with Sonia, decided she would continue caring for the children in both homes, primarily to preserve the positive relationship she had developed with the children.

Before the separation, Sonia was a "blank slate," refusing to take sides in their marital disputes. Sam recognized this and, although at times preferring Sonia to be more on his side of the dispute, respected her. It was better for the kids to have someone familiar with their family life who could be neutral when they had worries and concerns about their parents' behavior. But after the separation, living apart from Kathy and with little control over how she was conducting her personal life or care of the kids, Sam unwittingly created a new role for Sonia. She would become his eyes and ears, boots on the ground, about Kathy. Was there another man in Kathy's life? Who was he? Did he spend time with the kids? What was Kathy buying for the kids? Was it excessive? Would his childcare support increase because of this?

Nothing was ever said directly. Sam navigated around these hot-button questions, approaching them with a veiled interest in the well-being of the children. He almost hated himself for manipulating Sonia in this way, but wasn't this all about the kids and not about him?

Sonia was the level-headed individual to resolve this challenge. In characteristic style, she refused to take sides and she drew a line in the sand. She put Sam's concerns back where they belonged: in Sam and Kathy's lap. She simply said, "When you ask me these questions, I feel in the middle of a problem you have with Kathy. This is not a position I want to be in. Do you have a solution to get me out of the middle so you and Kathy can take care of the concerns you have about each other?"

LGBT AND
NANNIES

Nontraditional, LGBT[37] parents have become more commonplace in recent years, joining the ranks of traditional heterosexual parents in raising children. But this right to parent and the acceptance of doing "no harm" in the process hasn't happened easily. When it comes to hiring a nanny, the simple fact of being LGBT gives us sufficient pause. Questions unique to being considered a "nontraditional" parent factors into the hiring process and the nanny you select.

Hiring someone to help in the care and raising of children involves creating a worldview and defining values for your children that match your own. In the ideal world, we make choices about who we choose to be part of our lives, what values are transmitted, what the look and feel of life is that gives it meaning. For many parents, this includes a nanny.

For LGBT parents, the decision to raise children most often isn't an easy one. Only recently, social, cultural and legal norms have accepted LGBT individuals as having the right to parent. There is the stigma of mental health. It wasn't until 1987 that the *Diagnostic and Statistical Manual of Mental Disorders* (DSM-III-R), the bible of mental health professionals, eliminated the diagnosis of homosexuality as a mental health issue. There are the legal arguments. In 2015, the federal courts and many state legislatures overturned laws preventing LGBT individuals the right

---

37 *LGBT* in this section refers to all individuals under the umbrella of *LGBTQIA*.

to marry and right to parent[38]. There are the social norms. The idea that children should be raised in a nuclear family made up of a mother and a father prevails despite considerable data that indicates other family structures can be just as successful.[39] Finally, the idea that children raised in LGBT families would be harmed is a silent expectation in the hearts and minds of many individuals throughout cities and towns across America.[40]

For many LGBT individuals overcoming stigmas and opposition to claim their identity, the path to marrying and raising children has not been an easy one. Many have faced prejudices and had to carve out their own individual ways to manage decisions about family. They bring these experiences into their process about how to parent and, if this involves hiring a nanny, whom to choose.

In my work with LGBT families, there are several issues to address that are unique to their lifestyle.

1. *Acceptance:* You want your nanny to accept who you are as a parent and family. You want her to accept your role without gender stereotypes. Who is the "father" and who is the "mother" in this family are subtle culturally based questions. These are questions LGBT parents should answer for themselves. This will help guide you and your nanny as you face such questions from the larger society and instill acceptance in your child.

2. *Values:* While most LGBT families teach traditional values, how they teach these can be unique. For example, the "Golden Rule" can mean treating other types of families with the same respect you

---

38   http://www.msn.com/en-us/news/us/supreme-courts-landmark-ruling-legalizes-gay-marriage-nationwide/ar-AAcaBM5

39   http://www.frc.org/issuebrief/new-study-on-homosexual-parents-tops-all-previous-research

40   Results of research suggest that lesbian and gay parents are as likely as heterosexual parents to provide supportive home environments for children.
http://www.apa.org/pi/lgbt/resources/parenting.aspx

would like to receive. Teaching the importance of family includes defining what a family is.

3. *Lifestyle:* While all families need to keep boundaries around their personal lives in their nanny relationship, what can seem common among heterosexual couples, such as expressions of affection toward each other, can be a new and possibly awkward experience for a nanny working for an LGBT family. If two dads kiss each other routinely at the end of a workday, you want this to be "normal" and not "weird" or "icky." Your friends in the LGBT community may include an array of individuals that express their sexuality openly. You want your nanny to feel as comfortable among your friends as they would be having her with them.

Remember that your nanny will have her own history of experiences that may or may not match yours. Understanding and acceptance of different values, child-rearing customs and chosen lifestyle goes both ways. Everyone's acceptance of these differences is important.

Some questions LGBT parents may consider are these:

1. Do you want to hire a "manny" or a nanny?

2. How important is it that your nanny is LGBT or has worked with LGBT families before?

3. Who is the nanny in your family? What role does she play?

4. What about the questions strangers inevitably will ask your nanny: "Who is the mother/father?" What about those they will ask your child: "What is your mommy's name? What is your daddy's name?"

5. What about the questions your child may ask your nanny: "Who is my mommy?" "How come I don't have a daddy like Johnny does?"

These questions and others you will discover along your journey of parenting have no right or wrong answers. They simply become important jumping-off points for further discussion, first among yourselves and subsequently during a nanny interview. In my experience, asking questions that can be answered "yes" or "no" can be reassuring but not confirming. A candidate can say she is okay working with a two-mom family, but how she might respond to expectable questions because she works with a two-mom family is important. Using your own life experiences, you may create situation questions like those above to ask candidates. Remember: there are no right or wrong answers. There can also be an awkward response or one that says, "I don't know how I would respond." The importance of the questions is to acknowledge the elephant in the room and find a way to discuss what inevitably will become part of the relationship you will create with your nanny.

JOHN AND KEITH'S STORY

A Gay Couple

John met Keith while working to legalize same-sex marriage in San Francisco. Keith had watched John, a civil rights attorney, argue before the courts about a gay man's constitutional right to marry. Keith was a community organizer, passionate and convincing in his speeches in front of hundreds of LGBT activists and facing an equal amount of backlash from dissenters. Initially it was John and Keith's unwavering beliefs that brought them together. Later their friendship bloomed into romance. In 2008 at City Hall in San Francisco, they married.

That they would create a family was clear from the start. Just as they were unwavering in their political and social beliefs, they were unwavering in their beliefs about parenthood. In 2009 they identified a surrogate, Keith went through fertility treatment and their daughter, Karin, was born in late 2011. John then adopted Karin and became a co-parent with full parental rights, as was the law in California.

John took three months' paternity leave and then Keith did the same. They rearranged their work schedules to care for Karin most days of the week, a job-sharing model they had experienced in their careers. They still needed childcare to cover the part of the week when they were both working or when they needed an extra hand around the house. Using the resources and connections they had made in the community, finding a pool of candidates was relatively easy. It was the "who" that became challenging.

As a couple working on a challenging issue in which they shared a common goal, communication about what they wanted or needed wasn't a problem they had to address. It was questions unique to their lifestyle and the market of nannies that were.

Should they hire a "manny" or a nanny? If they hired a nanny, how would their daughter understand who the nanny was in their family? Would Karin expect that the nanny is her mom? What about the strangers on the street or the baristas at Starbucks saying to the nanny naïvely, "What a beautiful girl you have! She looks just like you!" Their lesbian friends had told them stories about their nanny being asked by strangers, "Who is the dad?" John and Keith knew they couldn't prevent these questions, but they wanted to know from a candidate, how would you answer if asked?

There was yet another nagging issue—their relationship. John and Keith were a loving gay couple and, as heterosexual couples can be, they were quite affectionate toward each other. How would a nanny feel if Keith kissed John when he came home from work? Would it feel "icky" to her? Would she pray for their sins or hope for a conversion? Would she keep silent to her own family about their lifestyle, expecting some teasing or retribution if disclosed?

It was Keith who shed some light on these questions. Over the years in discussions with many people having passionate and differing points of view about LGBT rights, he had faced his own prejudices and stereotypes that challenged his ability to understand what it's like to be in someone else's shoes. He told John, "It's really less about the nanny and more about us. We need to better understand how we define ourselves, our roles as parents, our beliefs and values. We need to face our own prejudices and stereotypes based on gender, on culture and religious beliefs as we search for our nanny. We should expect that a great nanny for us can include someone with a very different lifestyle than ours and that she may have a learning curve as she begins to understand the idiosyncrasies of how we want to raise Karin. This is the only way we can truly know who a person is and how she can join our family life."

When Keith and John met Pema, they fell in love. She was refreshingly open and honest.

As Pema told her life story, they realized two distinguishing traits that would make her the right fit. She exuded joy as she held Karin and talked with warmth and knowledge about the many children she had cared for over the years. She also had adapted beautifully to the many challenges in her personal life. Born and raised in Tibet, Pema emigrated at a young age with her parents over the vast Himalayan range on foot. In Kathmandu, she found work caring for the infant daughter of an ex-pat, an American single mother on assignment for the U.S. Embassy. She cared for this girl there for six years and then emigrated with the family to the U.S., where she stayed on for the next three years until the child no longer needed care.

Along the way, Pema learned a different parenting style than the one in which she was raised. She was fascinated by the opportunities American children had that were not possible in Nepal or Tibet. She earned her green card, learned to drive and worked as much as possible to support her independent living in her newly adopted country. When John asked questions concerning their lifestyle, Pema answered with the following: "I've never worked with a gay family before, but it won't be a new experience. I live my life according to the Dalai Lama's teachings of acceptance and goodness in everyone." That was when Keith and John embraced their uniqueness and looked ahead to learning about Pema's.

WHAT DOES IT TAKE TO KEEP A NANNY ON THE JOB?

Most parents are so relieved to find and hire a nanny who fits their family that they overlook an essential part of the relationship: what it takes to keep her happy on the job. For parents, keeping a loving, knowledgeable and reliable nanny on the job is essential. Children need to trust that the nanny watching over them will stay for as long as their parents need childcare. Nannies need time to understand a child's temperament, idiosyncrasies and behavior. Parents need time to create a partnership with a nanny who will care for their child in a way that is similar enough to their style. It's all about relationships—and relationships take time to develop.

In the first months of employment parents and nannies often go through a sort of honeymoon period. They are excited to learn new things about the kids and about each other. Every day is a new adventure. The parents experience relief from some of their daily responsibilities with the kids and the nanny experiences (often) the satisfaction of meeting the behavioral challenges as the kids learn to trust her more. And then everyone gets into the routine of daily life and the efficiencies of knowing what comes next. Communication gets easier, familiar and often occurs in shorthand form. Whether it's the parents running out the door in the morning with a quick, "He didn't sleep well last night—he'll probably be cranky today," or a stay-at-home mom saying to her nanny, "Would you mind grabbing a few things out of the fridge for our lunch while I breast-feed Johnny?" there's an unstated understanding about how things should go.

These efficiencies have a double edge. On the one hand, it is reassuring to know the family life and childcare are going smoothly. On the other hand, it doesn't give one an opportunity to anticipate and plan for changes. Is it time to childproof the house because Sophia will start walking soon? Do we have to be more careful when diapering Johnny on the changing table because he'll start rolling over any day now? When time passes by efficiently and quickly, so do the anniversary dates of when nannies were hired. Market changes in salaries also go unnoticed. Any changes in the amount of responsibilities a nanny takes on or how well she does them often get overlooked.

There's also a level of intimacy in the parent-nanny relationship that evolves over time. When the individual you invited into your home becomes an observer and to some degree a participant in the intimacies of your personal life, walking the boundary between employer and the personal warrants attention. A nanny can be privy to marital conflicts, separations and divorce or the intimacies of LGBT couples that may run counter to what she experiences in her personal life. Your nanny may get easily caught in the middle of conflicts between couples, pulled by either side to show preferences about who is the better parent to the child they are equally responsible for.

Rather than leaving the relationship to chance, I recommend taking a proactive and deliberate approach to keeping your nanny satisfied and engaged. It's not possible to prevent problems from entering the nanny-parent-child relationship, but it is quite possible to keep them to a minimum! In my years of experience, I've found that families that establish best practices and adhere to these have relationships with their nannies that keep them satisfied and on the job. These best practices fall into categories I call the 4C's:

1. Collaborate

2. Communicate

3. Compensate a livable wage

4. Continue education and support

Best Practices to Keep Nannies on the Job

First C - Collaborate

Effective collaboration between nannies and parents is essential, but it doesn't happen without planning and forethought. While "winging it" might work for the rare few, my experience shows that giving thought to how you want to team with your nanny and putting the appropriate structure in place to support that collaboration underpins the most successful nanny-parent relationships.

Defining how you will collaborate is important. It will clarify your role and responsibility vis-à-vis your nanny. Here are some options to consider:

1. You give direction daily and your nanny follows these instructions. She reports when things don't go as expected.

2. You give responsibility to your nanny to determine how the care will go when she is in charge, based on your training and input. Your nanny checks in regularly and gives suggestions on how to resolve problems when they occur. You discuss options, but you are the final decision-maker.

3. You give your nanny complete charge of your child's care when she is caring for him, with guidelines and direction from you. Your nanny reports only those situations you determine require your attention. You are the decision-maker.

These are just a few examples; there are various permutations and combinations of how parents collaborate. The important message is to tackle the question up front and make your wishes known to your nanny.

Collaboration is fundamental to the working relationship between a parent and nanny. Knowing how your child is being cared for and is responding to that care cannot be overlooked or underestimated.

Eight Ways to Establish Collaboration with Your Nanny

1. Use a contract.

As discussed in Chapter 15, contracts are essential to clarify expectations about the terms of your working relationship. They go a long way toward resolving problems when misunderstandings arise. A contract sets the boundaries of your working relationship. You are the employer and your nanny is your employee. It establishes the parent as the authority to make decisions.

2. Establish clear and reasonable expectations.

Nannies should know what their responsibilities are, how they are to be performed and when. Who makes decisions about where your child goes every day? While you may want your nanny to bring your child to various activities, you may want to be in charge of where he goes and give daily instructions to your nanny about this. Some parents prefer that the nanny take responsibility for researching what is available and implement the plan. How do you want to be apprised of what's happening during the day? Some parents want video and text reports; others simply don't have the time or don't want this high level of interaction. Remember: most parents set and reset expectations over time as they learn what works best for them and what is reasonable for the nanny to do.

SUSIE'S STORY

Susie called, completely baffled and frustrated. "How did I get into this mess?" she asked. She had assumed that Roberta would bring her own food to work every day, but it seemed Roberta had a different expectation. In Roberta's experience, her employer had the responsibility for providing all meals and beverages while working. Well, this was quite a surprise—and an expensive one—to Susie. Every day Roberta would stop by a local purveyor of fine foods and using the "kitty money" Susie had set aside for activities and emergencies, purchase a nice lunch for herself. Susie wanted to handle this head-on but didn't want to get into the awkward position of being considered cheap or viewing Roberta as entitled. Susie knew they were both responsible for making assumptions and for solving the problem. After a straightforward discussion, Susie agreed to give a reasonable stipend for food and Roberta agreed to pay for anything over and above. They set aside a "Roberta-only" section in the pantry for her food supplies and Roberta agreed not to raid the refrigerator of certain items set aside for Susie and her family.

3. Set priorities.

The expectations many parents have for their nanny is that she provides safe, responsible care for their child, perform the light housecleaning related to his care and run errands if and when it's possible. But simply listing these can be a setup for failure unless you prioritize what's important. No two days are alike in a child's world! When kids get sick, for example, getting the laundry done may be impossible. When a tired parent comes home from work and sees the laundry undone and a sick, cranky child being soothed, it helps on both sides if everyone is clear that on days like this the laundry can't get done.

4. Provide training.

It's surprising how easy it is for parents to forget that it takes time and effort to learn how to get through the daily routines of their child's life. Parents fail to remember how much detail gets stored in the schemata of their minds in order to do what they do automatically every day. The baby wakes up around 6 a.m. You fill the bottle with so much formula, pop the bottle in the warmer, go in and change his diaper, put on his favorite onesie plus a hat because he gets cold easily, pick him up and carry him to the kitchen, get the bottle, unplug the warmer, go to the rocker in the living room and feed him five ounces before he needs to be burped. He likes to be held this way and usually will burp in a minute or so if you pat his back this way . . .

Well, you get the idea. There's a lot of detail in the simple routines and we haven't discussed the other important details: what needs to be prepared just to go out for the daily walk at 10 a.m.; where everything is kept; how to get the stroller, the diaper bag *and* baby down the stairs to go for the walk; the route you usually take to get back home before he gets cranky so he sleeps in his bed instead of in the stroller.

It can seem that "what moms just do" clouds the reality that nannies, just like all new employees, need some on-the-job training. In general, training takes one to two weeks during which your nanny learns the routines and idiosyncrasies of your child, finds out where everything is in the house related to his care and learns about the neighborhood walks, parks, shops, libraries and other places you regularly visit that are safe and kid friendly.

Don't forget to train your nanny in how to handle medical emergencies, police/fire safety situations and disasters.

A document called "Emergency Procedures Training for Nanny" is included at the back of this book and/or can be downloaded from The Institute for Families and Nannies website: http://www.tiffan.org

5. Learn where your nanny shines—and doesn't.

One of the most valuable aspects of training your nanny is learning where she shines and where she doesn't. Let's face it, even the nanny that is so right for your family can't be 100 percent right in everything! And it's always better to recognize these traits early on in the relationship, as you discover them. If Rosalind isn't meticulous about putting the folded laundry away on the right shelf in the closet, then you might need to get over your disappointment when you find Michael's socks in Robert's part of the closet. Remember that some things won't change in a nanny's character. While this might be a constant irritation, better to shrug it off as "there she goes again!" than get worked up and nag, criticize and neglect all the wonderful things she does to make your life easier.

6. Teach what is teachable and accept what isn't.

The benefit of recognizing your nanny's Achilles' heel up front is that you'll have a better chance of shaping the outcome. If you know where your nanny's strengths lie and where she can use some support, everyone is in a better position to succeed. With this approach, there are no secrets, elephants in the room or walking on eggshells among the adults! Everyone shares ideas about how to improve things, knows what works and, in spite of everyone's good intentions, knows what just isn't going to change.

7. Teach your child that you trust your nanny.

Training is often thought of as teaching your nanny about your child, the house and the neighborhood. But what about your child? What does your child need to learn about the nanny?

It is so essential that your child understand that you trust this stranger before leaving him with her!

We've spent a lot of time discussing how important it is that you trust your nanny to do right by you and your child. You called references and had meaningful discussions with her to ensure that she is who she says she is and will care for your child safely. Well, your child has the same worry—who is this person and how will she know what I want and need? How will she respond? Will I like her? How could my mom possibly leave me with someone I've known for such a short period of time?

The best way for your child to learn to trust your nanny is to learn that *you* trust your nanny.

With very young children, that can be accomplished by caring for your baby side-by-side, unrushed, talking about what he likes and dislikes, what makes him happy, the challenges you encounter with him and the hopes you have for him. For preschool-age children, introducing your nanny as someone who "really likes kids and knows a lot about kids and what makes them happy" sends them a neutral and meaningful message. With a child that needs time to warm up, you can pave the way by saying, "Monica is a new person. It takes time to get to know her." And "Mommy is going to tell Monica all about you so she can get to know you too!"

Spend as much time together as possible. If you are transitioning from one nanny to another, have them spend time together with your child. He will learn that his nanny also trusts the new nanny.

FLORENCE'S STORY

Florence was a private person and reluctant to have Arlie train the new nanny. What if Arlie gossips and tells stories about things that didn't go so well in their relationship? Florence didn't want Arlie to influence the new relationship in negative ways. What to do? Florence gave Arlie the task to create a document, "Arlie's Tips and Tricks," to instruct the new nanny on how to navigate the daily routines and particular behaviors of her daughter, Amy. This included such information as "What I like most about Amy. What Amy enjoys. What she doesn't like. The three hopes I have for her care." Transitioning and training in this way solved Florence's worry about gossiping, respected her need for privacy and transferred essential information about Amy to the new nanny from the person responsible for her care until then.

8. Expect differences in style and respect them.

You may recall the discussion about values earlier in this book illustrating how values are learned and influence relationships. It's interesting to note how one common value, respecting authority, can creep into the parent-nanny relationship and influence the degree to which collaboration happens. Many nannies were raised and achieved success adhering to the value of respecting authority. This doesn't necessarily imply deference or compliance; but for some nannies it does present a challenge when it comes to collaboration. Nannies may feel they don't have the right to be forthcoming about their ideas or opinions. It's not that they don't have them; it's more that they need permission from their employer to share them. Establishing collaboration may mean a respectful and constant reminder to your nanny that her ideas are welcomed and important. We will revisit this in the section on communication later in this chapter, as it also affects a nanny's style of communicating.

Second C - Communicate

If there are commonalities among nannies about what constitutes a good job for them, communication is first on the list. Nannies say they want to be "on the same page" as parents. Being respected for what they know and do comes in as a close second. The message is a simple one: communication and respect ensure job satisfaction.

Today everyone is texting and using apps to communicate. It's easy, quick and an inexpensive way to keep in touch. Sending video text messages is almost always welcomed. Want to keep track of the daily feeding, sleeping, playing, peeing and pooping routines? There's an app for that! Need everyone to be on top of scheduling hours, activities and special events? Set up and manage a Google calendar! This is the great age of sharing information and you can be as "high-touch" as you want. Simply set up the system, advise your nanny and adjust as needed.

Effective communication, however, is not so easily achieved by implementing a high-tech system of communication. A tweet, a text message or an email can't easily capture the complexities of a situation when there is a lot at stake in the outcome. When nannies were asked to rate the most difficult conversation to have with their employer, the majority rated these in the following order:

- Money

- Scheduling

- Child's behavior

There are obvious reasons why these topics are so difficult. Nannies are worried about the outcome. Will they be fired for asking for a raise or complaining about the changing schedule or the hours that have become too long? Will they be seen as incompetent if they have a problem managing the child's behavior? Will the parents feel that the nanny is critical of their parenting skills, suggesting they are bad parents or that their child has "problems"? Better to keep these concerns to themselves and preserve their job and goodwill.

Parents have their own challenges in effectively communicating with their nanny. These range from not having the time to communicate to being worried about the outcome if their nanny becomes upset with them. There's always the possibility of dissonance in communication styles. If you're a direct, no-nonsense communicator working with a nanny who is compliant and likes to please, your directness could be interpreted as anger or dissatisfaction with her job performance. And then there are those nasty feelings no one wants to admit have crept back into the parent-nanny relationship: guilt, inadequacy and denial. As a *New York Times* article noted:

"*Many mothers who employ nannies are actually overstretched working women, a number of whom (contrary to their professional personas) suffer from an inability to clearly express their expectations and demands to the people they pay to care for their children. The result is a peculiar passive-aggressive form of communication, a less-than-ideal dynamic between worker and boss. The mother, at times beset by guilt, a touch of intimidation or feelings of her own maternal inadequacy, fails to articulate what she wants from the nanny—and then complains to friends, her spouse or an Internet message board when she doesn't get it. (The father in many cases steers clear of the whole relationship.)*[41]

As a result, a parent may leave the responsibility of communicating to their nanny who is expected to figure out and bring up issues that need discussion. As we have noted above, many nannies have their own problems talking to their employers. The result can range from denial of the problem to passive-aggressive behavior that often gets played out in a way that leaves everyone wondering what the problem is and how they got there.

---

41   Hilary Stout, "How to Speak Nanny," *The New York Times*, February 3, 2010.

SYLVIA'S STORY

Sylvia was not happy with the raise her employers gave when their second child was born. She avoided a direct discussion, expecting the parents would think she was asking for too much and would hire someone else. Her disappointment, combined with frustration, led to an assumption that the parents didn't respect her. Surely, they would know what she was worth. The result: Sylvia's attitude and job performance changed. She no longer was available to work additional hours. She started to come late for work. The dishes were often left in the sink. Her employers interpreted this as Sylvia not having the skills or interest to care for more than one child. Clearly, she was not as on top of things as she had been before the baby was born. They moved to hire someone else, realizing in the process that they had to pay a higher salary. They justified this as paying more for a more qualified person. Sylvia interpreted their decision as confirmation of their lack of respect for the value she could bring to their family.

TRISH'S STORY

When Trish interviewed Lina, she said she could prepare baby food. Trish assumed that she would—not just that she could. Two months later when her son started eating solid food, Trish was surprised when Lina asked where the baby food was. Trish interpreted the question as "parents provide the food and nannies feed the baby." This led to the assumption "surely we misinterpreted what Lina said she would do when we interviewed her." Trish avoided asking for clarification. She had heard too many stories from her friends about their nannies grumbling about having to do too much work in addition to caring for the child. Surely, she didn't want a cranky nanny on her hands. So on weekends, Trish and her husband spent their precious time together cutting, steaming, pureeing and freezing veggies in ice-cube trays so Lina could have fresh baby food ready when needed. Grumbling, they would say to each other, "I can't believe we're doing this! What are we paying Lina all our hard-earned money to do anyway? She sits and reads a book while he naps for three hours every day—and we puree baby food on weekends! Something is wrong here!"

JESSICA'S STORY

Jessica was a millennial nanny, raised by parents in a culture that taught her she could be anything she wanted and have whatever she wanted. Growing up, everything she did received accolades. "That was awesome!" "Great job!" "You are amazing!" When she competed in school, everyone received a prize so no one would feel left out or inadequate. In her early 20s, Jessica wanted to make a difference in the world. She was exuberant and confident that she could change things and had the skills to do this. When she took a nanny position with the Smith family's two elementary school children, she agreed to work alongside Tania to manage the daily household responsibilities and the children's after-school care. She expected this would include planning and developing age-appropriate activities for the children and creating an organized system of household chores and an inventory of household supplies that would run things efficiently. Tania, however, had a different expectation. She needed someone to pitch in and do the "mom stuff." Beds had to be made, laundry done, grocery shopping and errands run. Meals had to be prepared. Last-minute changes had to be navigated. The kids had to be picked up and transported "soccer-mom" style. Six months after Jessica started she gave a two-day notice that she was leaving. She didn't feel awesome in her job and wasn't making an impact. Tania liked Jessica. She told her they could figure out what would make Jessica feel fulfilled on the job. With patience, slowly and steadily, they could learn from each other what mattered. Hopefully the journey would be rewarding for both.

In my experience, there are three areas that can influence how effectively parents communicate with their nanny. These are character traits, cultural values and socioeconomic differences.

Character Traits: There's a body of research investigating differences among individuals in how they communicate and how these differences can affect interactions with others. Many psychologists have studied behavior traits such as dominance, submission and compliance, and while there are differences of opinion among the academics as to how these traits play out, there's no question that when it comes to parents and nannies, even the best of intentions can be misinterpreted.

GLORIA'S STORY

Gloria was unbelievably stressed out! Their new home was under construction, the holidays were two weeks away, the kids had gymnastics rehearsals for an upcoming competition and her husband had committed them to weekend holiday parties with business associates. On top of this craziness, he had an international business trip this week and was gone for three days. Sonia walked in that morning just as Tania was fielding calls from contractors and the kids were having a meltdown. Gloria turned and yelled to Sonia, "Get the kids under control and dressed for school! They need to leave in 10 minutes or they'll be late." Gloria didn't have time to be "nice." She thought Sonia would let this roll off her back and know that it was just a rotten day. She didn't expect that Sonia would feel bad; that she thought maybe she did something wrong the day before and that Gloria was mad at her.

Cultural Values: As discussed earlier in the section on collaboration, cultural values provide a road map about what is meaningful to people who are part of a group. It is useful to recognize how certain values affect communication between nannies and parents.

CELIA'S STORY

Celia grew up in a culture where respecting those in authority indicated you were raised well and would get ahead. You were polite, knew your place and followed the rules. Employers could hire you reassured that your work ethic would be strong and you would be loyal. These values got Celia out of her impoverished village and to America, where she worked as a nanny for a wealthy family. Celia rarely asked for anything. She trusted her employer would know her worth and do right by her. One day at the park, she overheard other nannies talking about their salaries. She was shocked that they were making much more than she. Celia felt somewhat betrayed by the values she stood by and that had done so well by her. She also recognized that in America, the value of respect for authority could include telling your employer what's on your mind. But Celia was in a bind. She'd never had a conversation like this with any employer. How could she begin to have such a difficult conversation while also keeping her integrity?

Socioeconomic Differences: Although no reliable data exists to describe the socioeconomic differences between parents and nannies, it is widely understood that the differences are vast. For nannies, their work environments can be constant reminders of what they can only wish for but not attain. Their feelings about these differences can range from envy to jealousy, inadequacy or entitlement. Likewise, parents recognize these differences and can construct a relationship with their nanny in a way to manage and navigate their own feelings, which often include guilt.

It is not a parent's responsibility to amend these areas of potential conflict. It is simply important to know they can exist and take these into consideration when a difficult conversation needs to happen.

Finally, effective communication with your nanny includes the precious individual you are both caring for: your child. In situations that involve understanding and managing your child's behavior, look at the problem behavior from your child's point of view, create a partnership with your nanny and look for a place to compromise. Here's an example to guide you along the way:

KRISTA'S STORY

It started happening when Charlie was about 18 months old. Krista would come home from work and expect Charlie to do as he always did—run excitedly to see her. Instead, Charlie would ignore Krista and keep playing with his puzzles. Once when Mara was playing with him, Charlie refused to go to Krista. He yelled, "No! Stay with Mara!" and ran to hide under the table, screaming the whole time. Krista was embarrassed, angry and felt like a bad mother. Mara told her it was because Charlie had a hard time making changes. Even though Krista hated to come home after a long day and face Charlie's resistance, she understood what Mara said. She experienced similar behavior when she was with Charlie on the weekends. He couldn't readily stop what he was doing and move on to the next thing. He seemed to need time to make a transition. At this age in particular, Charlie needed to feel like he was in charge of any situation.

Now it's time to have the conversation!

Eight Key Tips for Communicating Effectively with Your Nanny

1. Recognize something needs to be discussed.

2. Notice how you are feeling—keeping strong negative feelings in check.

3. Plan for the right setting.

4. State the problem and how you perceive it.

5. Provide options and solutions.

6. Expect the same from your nanny.

7. Agree on a solution and/or path forward.

8. Set a time to follow up.

Here's an example: Your nanny consistently arrives five or ten minutes late for work. Knowing you don't want this to continue, you decide to address it before it becomes habitual. You know your nanny well enough that having an honest and direct conversation works best. You have some ideas about what can be done so she arrives on time, but you recognize she most likely has ideas herself. You also want to have the discussion without rushing, know that it can't happen with the kids and don't want her wondering what the discussion will be about. You email or text her to stay 15 minutes at the end of one day that week for a discussion about her schedule. With the children in another room, you start the conversation:

"You've been working for me now for almost four months and I'm very happy with how you're taking care of Sam. Every time I come home he's clean, happy and doesn't want you to go home! So, thanks for making my life easier on this account. At the same time, I've realized you're the type of person who always runs late. For example, for the past two weeks you've come to work five or ten minutes late four times. Every time you are late, I get stuck in traffic and am late for work. This not only gets me in a bad mood but in trouble with my employer. Is there something we can do to be sure you are here on time? Would it help if you set your alarm to wake up earlier or for us to set your start time here earlier?"

Third C - Compensate a Livable Wage

In 2016, Marcy Whitebook, a professor at U.C. Berkeley, reported on the travesty of low earnings for preschool teachers with early childhood education (ECE) compared with pre-K teachers.   She noted:

"Despite all we have learned about the crucial development in the first years of life and the important role of teachers in facilitating early learning, ECE jobs offer little premium to those teachers who have earned degrees. ECE has the dubious distinction of affording graduates the lowest lifetime earnings of any college major. As was true a quarter century ago, teachers with four-year degrees employed in Head Start and many public pre-K programs earn between 60 and 70 percent of the average kindergarten teacher salary. These low-paying jobs often do not offer benefits or professional supports, such as paid time for planning, reflection and professional development."[42]

Supporting Dr. Whitebook's findings, the Early Childhood Workforce Index in 2016 reported that early educators are among the lowest-paid workers in the country. The median hourly wages for childcare workers range from $8.72 in Mississippi to $12.24 in New York. Nationwide, the median wage is $9.77. Preschool teachers fare somewhat better:

---

[42]   Marcy Whitebook, "It is time to change how we prepare and support early childhood educators," Bill and Melinda Gates Foundation, October 19, 2015.

wages range from $10.54 in Idaho to $19.21 in Louisiana. In contrast, the median national wage for kindergarten teachers is $24.83.[43]

Do nannies fare better than other early educators nationally? According to a 2016 survey conducted by the online organization PayScale[44], the average nanny salary nationally is 27 percent less than that of the highest wage earners nationally among preschool teachers.[45]

While it is not the purpose of this book to advocate for higher wages for nannies, this information is meaningful, as it informs how paying a livable wage impacts how long a nanny stays on the job and the quality of care a nanny provides.

In the 1995 landmark study on Cost, Quality and Childcare Outcomes[46] in childcare center settings, investigators examined what made for quality of care in these centers across the U.S. Results showed the following five indicators affect quality of care.

1. Group size

2. Staff-child ratios

3. Salaries

4. Turnover rates

---

43   Marcy Whitebook, Caitlin McLean and Lea Austin, The Early Childhood Workforce Index: State of the Early Childhood Workforce, Center for the Study of Child Care Employment, July 7, 2016.

44   http://www.payscale.com/research/US/Job=Nanny/Hourly_RateCountry: United States | Currency: USD | Updated: 28 Oct 2016 | Individuals Reporting: 5,195

45   This percentage may be misleading to families living in large urban areas, as nanny salaries there are higher than the national average and more closely resemble salaries among preschool teachers in those areas. According to a 2017 survey by Glassdoor, the average salary for a nanny in San Francisco is $43,738. This is 59.7% higher than the national median salary of $27,392. These figures also fail to account for the reality that many nannies are paid "under-the-table" or nontaxable income.

46   Suzanne W. Helburn, Cost, Quality and Child Outcomes in Child Care Centers, Technical Report, Public Report, and Executive Summary, University of Colorado, Denver, 1995.

5. Continued education and training

These findings were interpreted to mean that if group size and childcare ratios were low, a childcare worker was paid a livable wage and received continued education and support, then turnover rates would be low. Low turnover rates affect the quality of care children receive, as it allows the opportunity for a trusting relationship between the childcare worker and child to develop. Having a trusting relationship with an adult responsible for a child's care is the foundation for healthy development.

While this type of study has not been replicated in the nanny industry, the results do prompt us to reflect on whether similar outcomes can occur. Until such a study is conducted, assumptions must be made to answer two meaningful and very important questions: What keeps a nanny on the job? What makes for quality care by a nanny?

The assumptions one must make when comparing outcomes from the Cost, Quality and Child Outcomes study to the nanny industry are these: Given that a nanny, by definition, cares for a small group of children and that the adult-child ratio is low, then these two indicators of quality from the study can be left out of the question. This leaves three indicators to be investigated: salary, continued education/support and turnover rates. From there, this question can be formed: To what degree do these three indicators affect quality of care from a nanny? Commonsense reasoning suggests that paying a livable wage keeps nannies on the job and reduces turnover rates. Providing continued education/support gives a nanny a set of skills to provide informed care, which may affect job satisfaction and keep the nanny on the job longer than the average nanny tenure. Taken together—or separately—both indicators are likely to keep nannies on the job. Retaining a nanny allows for a trusting relationship between the child and nanny to develop.

Parents who fail to pay a livable wage or who fail to pay wages for work performed increase the risk of turnover. Nannies leave for better pay and better working conditions. In turn, it can be expected that high turnover rates among nannies affect quality of care. A child who is cared for by a revolving door of nannies, each of whom leaves too soon, simply doesn't have the opportunity to develop a trusting relationship with an adult responsible for the child's care.

Fourth C - Continue Education and Training

When I started my work with families and nannies, I was impressed with how much nannies knew about how to care for young children. Many of these had no formal education or training to learn their "craft." I was tempted to conclude that early childhood education and training was not needed to provide informed, loving care. It was also tempting to expect that maternal instinct held sway—that women[47] were born with an innate ability to care for children and to do this well.

My experience working with parents reinforced these ideas. Comparing nannies who possessed formal early childhood education as well as warmth to nannies who were warm but had no such education, most parents chose the latter. Their thinking? Nannies don't need formal early childhood education to provide loving, warm and knowledgeable care.

These expectations defied reason. They also defied the norms one sees in other professions. When an employer recruits a worker to perform a skill at a high level, hiring decisions are often based on the amount and quality of education and training the candidate has. Why was this different among parents hiring a nanny? Does early childhood

---

47   According to the U.S. Bureau of Labor Statistics, just 2.3 percent of preschool and kindergarten teachers are male. http://www.tolerance.org/blog/accounting-missing-men-early-childhood

education matter? To what degree does early childhood education and support affect quality of care?

These questions remain vitally important to our understanding, yet remain unanswered to date by any study investigating the quality of care provided by nannies. One is left to rely on common sense, reasoning and experience.

Assuming nannies with higher education and training are also warm and attentive, education and training can inform the care they provide. These nannies can base their decisions about what to do, how to do it and why on their formal training. They also have the ability to talk about why they responded to the child in a certain way rather than simply acting through experience or instinct alone.

Is formal early childhood education the only way one can learn the "craft" of childcare? Again, commonsense reasoning implies that it is not. Informal support networks and learning from observation and through discussions with others are some of the many other ways nannies learn their "craft." Some nannies are avid readers of parenting books and scour the internet for ideas about child development and behavior.

In 2014, my colleague Ahava Vogelstein and I began monthly continuing education and training for nannies. We covered a range of topics from child development, literacy, challenging behavior, and sibling rivalry to the importance of play. Several highly knowledgeable nannies facilitated some of these workshops in subject areas they were knowledgeable about. What we learned was fascinating. Nannies were interested in learning from us about the material but equally interested in learning from each other. They benefited not only by gaining insight, knowledge and skills, but also from learning the words and language to describe what they were doing.

"So what do you do when Carrie has a meltdown in the supermarket?" we ask a nanny named Maggie. "Well, first of all, I just try to get there before she gets tired or hungry 'cause I know if she is, I'm asking for trouble. Sometimes, boy, she really gets into a fit, crying like crazy to get something she knows she can't have! When she gets that way there's no reasoning with her. I just wait there next to her; sometimes if she lets me, I'll hold on to her while she's sobbing 'cause I know it calms her down. Then when she's finished, I just look her in the eye and tell her I know she's tired and we should probably just get home for some rest. Maybe we can get the milk we needed before we go or else we can just go right away. Usually she says 'get the milk, okay?' On the ride home, she usually falls sound asleep. She's so exhausted." "That's what they call 'connect before you correct,'" we tell her. Maggie is pleased. She likes knowing what she's been doing all these years has a name and that others who do research on how kids learn agree with what she's doing.

What does this mean for parents who want to keep their nanny on the job? Learning how children develop and mastering a range of skills around how to support development is interesting, enriching and can be exciting for nannies. It professionalizes their work and informs what they do. This type of learning can happen formally in early childhood education classes or informally through networking and support groups with other caregivers, by direct observation and discussions with others, through internet research, and by reading books and magazines about child development and behavior.

Four Ways to Support Your Nanny's Continued Learning

1. Recognize that learning is important and informs the care your nanny provides.

2. Encourage your nanny to attend classes, workshops and trainings on child development and care. Bring that learning back into the relationship with you and your child.

3. Encourage your nanny to start an informal nanny support/learning group.

4. Call in the experts: know when outside consultation to manage difficult behavior is needed. Include your nanny in the learning.

What Does It Take to Keep a Parent in Charge? Prepare for the Unexpected

Even if you have a nanny in place with clear expectations, issues will arise when you're least prepared for them. Being mindful of common pitfalls and planning ahead for what might happen will help keep you in charge and in the driver's seat. Here are some areas to be watchful for:

1. Who is this person and why is she here?

While you may have a definition of who your nanny is and why she is there, you can't expect the same from your child. Imagine you are three months old and all you know is that this person called nanny comes to your house regularly and takes care of you. She leaves at the end of the day and goes somewhere, only to return again and again. Who is this person and where does she go? Children are very perceptive and it helps for parents to talk about what's going on around them, even to the youngest of children.

Here are some questions kids might ask their nanny and some ideas to guide you and your nanny in thinking about them. Remember there is never a "right" or "wrong" answer and, based on the age of your child and idiosyncrasies, less is always more! Children are very curious, and asking open-ended questions can reveal a world of ideas and more questions you may have not thought possible!

Question: Can you live in our house? *This question is often a child's way of figuring out who is family and where family lives.*

Answer: I have my own house, where I live with my family. You live with your family in this house. What would it be like if I lived in your house?

Question: Do you have a job? *This can be a way for young children to make sense of the world and work. While most adults have a very complex understanding of what comprises work and having a job, children are developing theirs.*

Answer: I have a job taking care of children. Right now I'm taking care of you. Do you know other people that have a job taking care of children?

Question: Do you have kids? *This can be another way of figuring out who their nanny is.*

Answer: Yes, I have two kids. Their names are John and Amy. John is grown up and Amy is in college now. Why did you ask? Imagine if I didn't have kids. What would that be like?

Question: Why is your skin brown? *This question is often a child's way of understanding differences among those in his world.*

Answer: My skin is brown because I belong to a group of people that live in a place called St. Croix. Do you know other people with a different color of skin than yours? How are they like you? How are they different?

2.   Where did my nanny go?

Imagine you are a little person and this adult comes to your house every day or regularly. One day she doesn't come. A long time passes and she still doesn't come. You begin to wonder—where did she go? Why isn't she here like before? Did something happen to her? Did I do something to make her go away?

Children notice when there's a change in what is expectable, particularly when they are not in charge of the change. They try to make sense of what is different. In their own way, based on experience, they give meaning to the event.

As the adult responsible for the change, whether initiated by you or not, you must help your child understand why his nanny isn't there anymore.

Here are some possible scenarios and answers to consider:

1. Your child starts preschool and doesn't need a nanny anymore. Answer: *"You are getting bigger and going to school every day. Your teacher at school will be taking good care of you during the day when I can't. Your nanny, Maria, will start taking care of another child who needs her now."*

2. You no longer need a nanny. Answer: *"Mommy doesn't need Maria to help her take care of you. Maria will start taking care of another child whose mommy needs help."*

3. You decided to hire a different nanny. Answer: *"Mommy decided Suzie is the right nanny to take care of you now. Maria will start taking care of another child whose mommy decided Maria is the right nanny for her child."*

Be prepared for possible reactions from your child that can range from matter-of-fact acceptance to protest. If your child protests, keep the message clear and simple. Listen and understand. Watch your feelings. Keep these neutral and focus on the positives. Stay the course. Remember, regardless of how your child responds to your nanny leaving, your child is learning how to say goodbye to an adult that has been part of her world. Saying goodbye is something everyone does throughout life. Learning to do this positively is an important lesson.

DEBBIE'S STORY

Elizabeth was taking care of Isaac every day and she really enjoyed it. But his mom, Debbie, was completely fed up with Elizabeth. Every time she told her to do something, it was never done right. She was tired of having to remind Elizabeth and was frustrated and angry. She felt she was paying Elizabeth to work for her and that Elizabeth was taking advantage of her. It got so bad that the two barely communicated.

One day when Debbie came home after work, she took Isaac and left the room with him. Isaac looked at his mom and Elizabeth anxiously. He didn't get a chance to say good-bye to Elizabeth, whom he adored. The next morning when he woke up, Elizabeth didn't come. She didn't come ever again. Isaac figured that when people are mad at each other, one of them goes away and doesn't come back.

3.   Don't leave me!

These are probably some of the most difficult and heartbreaking words a child can say to a parent. No matter how stoic, a parent's emotions can run amok. Is someone causing harm? Is it my nanny? Or is it me for leaving?

Here are some "rule out" questions to understand why your child protests when you leave.

Note: If you have an understanding about why the protests occur, then find the needed ideas and support from your nanny and other responsible adults to resolve them. If the protests continue, seek professional help and support.

1. Is this a developmental issue? Children generally protest when a parent leaves starting at 12 months and continuing until 30 months. This is the phase when they are learning that those they are closely attached to can leave and also return. This certainly includes parents, whether they go into the other room and are out of sight or go out and don't return for a period of time. Children can be different in the degree to which they protest. Some children cling and whimper; others scream and pound the door. With a good nanny, children learn how to say good-bye (waving at the window helps) and with some soothing, and reassurances that you will come back, return to play.

2. Has there been a change in your child's life? A new sibling, new home, new school or new nanny can generate protest from the most well-adjusted child. If there are multiple changes occurring at the same time, this increases the likelihood of protest. With time and support from caring adults, most children adjust.

3. Has there been an unusual incident in your child's life? A close examination of the relationships among important adults in the

child's life may be in order. For example, if you and your partner or spouse have been fighting or arguing lately, a child may worry that if you leave, you may not return.

4. Has there been a change in your working relationship with your nanny? If there has been tension or heated discussions with your nanny, your child may pick up on this. Why would you leave him with someone you don't trust?

5. Has there been a change in your nanny's behavior? If you suspect that your child is reacting to changes in your nanny's ability to provide safe, responsible and attentive care, then a discussion with her is in order to rule out harm to your child. Some parents choose to use their gut and let their nanny go without a discussion.

4.   Manipulation: Learning how to get what you want

Your nanny tells your child he can't have candy before dinner. You walk into the room and your child asks you if he can have some candy. You say, "Sure." Your child is very happy.

The next time this happens and your nanny says no, your child tells her it's okay because Mommy said so. Some nannies will hold their ground, saying, "Your Mommy told me when I'm taking care of you there's no candy. Just to be sure, I'll ask her again when she gets home," while others acquiesce. You come home and your child says your nanny gave him candy. Your nanny said you had agreed the other day, so she thought it was okay.

When kids are charming, when adults are tired, when expectations are left unclear and communication fails, then kids somehow manage to bend the rules. On most days, parents "pick their battles" and let it go. On other days, they hold the line.

If you want to stay in charge, it's best to address these manipulations and transgressions with your nanny. It can be as simple as, "I think he caught us off guard this time! What is that rule we had again?"

5.   Monday blues

For many nannies, Monday is the toughest day of the week. Why? Well, it often happens that on weekends, parents take a break from the rules and the kids do too! Those daily routines that set expectations about when and where the kids eat, sleep and play get out of whack. Often the junk food consumption level goes up as well! The result: cranky kids emerge from Monday morning sleep. Grumpy, overtired and fussy kids make for the Monday blues for nannies!

No parent should expect to curtail weekend fun and pleasure to make a nanny happy. But if you want to keep in charge of your nanny relationship, give her a heads-up about the Monday blues!

6.   Travel: Whose holiday is this anyway?

If there's one area of the parent-nanny relationship that is a mine field for problems, it's travel. Many nannies love to work for families that take them along when they travel. Who wouldn't want to have an all-expenses-paid trip to an exotic destination they've longed to visit? And to get paid to work while they are there? The allure is intoxicating.

And therein lies the problem for both the parent and the nanny. After all, parents bring their nanny because the parents want a vacation—and this means having someone help with the kids. They pay a good amount of their vacation budget to cover the cost of airfare, meals and hotel accommodations. And they pay for every hour the nanny works. Without question, as much as they love their nanny, they also expect she is working and not on vacation!

Nannies have their own expectations. The reality for most is that it can be like a vacation. Even though they are working, they are staying in a beautiful hotel, eating in a restaurant and having someone clean their room and make their bed every day. Even though they are working, when they are free they can explore or just have some downtime away from the routines of their daily life. Not a bad deal!

Even though this can be a win-win situation, sometimes there is a rocky start or things don't go well.

Here are some common scenarios for families traveling with nannies:

1. The parents and nanny have a clear conversation before the trip about compensation. The nanny knows she will be paid her usual rate and work at least the same number of hours she normally works, though the hours will be different. All expenses will be paid. When they return, the parents pay their nanny for all hours she worked. But it was a difficult international trip. The kids were jet-lagged and cranky and couldn't adjust. The nanny earned only slightly more than what she would normally earn if she stayed home. She refused to travel with them again. After some discussion, the parents told her the job required travel. If she chose not to go, she wouldn't be paid. They agreed, however, to pay a bonus for difficult travel.

2. The parents purchase airline tickets for their two children and nanny to fly economy while they enjoy the quieter pleasures of business class. It's a long flight and the kids want to see their parents. The nanny explains that their mom and dad are having a "date flight" and can't be disturbed. She gets them involved in having a date flight with their nanny.

3. The family goes to another country and stays at a five-star hotel in the center of the city. The nanny has never been to such a fancy hotel nor ever traveled abroad. She's not familiar with hotel services or getting around safely in an international city. When the parents

tell her to take care of the kids for the day, she stays in the hotel with the kids and doesn't venture beyond. The next day, the parents take her to the concierge and arrange for kid-friendly places she and the kids can go. They also go over safety rules for getting around in the city. Everyone discusses this that night at dinner.

4. The nanny shows up at the swimming pool in the resort wearing a very sexy bathing suit, orders a piña colada and flirts with the men around her. The kids show up with their parents at the pool. The kids want to run over and hang out with her. The parents are embarrassed and feel ashamed. The conservative nanny they left home with has turned into a stranger who no longer represents their family well.

5. The parents took their nanny on vacation knowing they wouldn't need much help but wanted the option. They would just play it by ear and let their nanny know when they needed her. Their nanny liked the idea and agreed to stay close by at the hotel and wait to hear from them. Every day, the nanny ordered room service for breakfast and expensive dinners poolside. She was around, but never did she ask the parents if she could be helpful. The parents would often see her at the pool or jogging on the beach and she would wave to them and ask, "Are you having fun?" At the end of the week, the nanny had worked half her normal schedule. When the taxi took everyone back from the airport, the nanny said good-bye and left. She didn't say she'd had a good time or thank them. The next day, the nanny called in sick. She said she was tired and jet-lagged.

6. Every summer the family went to the grandparents' summer home for two weeks. It was family time, with everyone together. This year, the parents took their nanny. The grandparents were getting older and the extra help would be welcomed. The nanny would stay in the guest room and share the bathroom with the kids. Two days

after everyone arrived, the grandparents said the nanny had to stay somewhere else. Family was family, and that didn't include the nanny. While the parents were okay with the decision, they hadn't budgeted the expense of a hotel room. This led to an awkward discussion with the grandparents. Everyone came to a solution, but it did somewhat sour the vacation.

Putting it All Together: Creating Relationships that Last

If there is a singular message, it is this: Relationships matter. Nannies create relationships with the children they care for and with the parents. The quality of these relationships determines how well the care goes, and often for how long.

Creating a quality relationship does require some attention to what happens in the parent-nanny-child relationship and keeping the lines of communication open and clear. It also requires acknowledgment that your child will have a relationship with your nanny that will be unique to them and possibly very different from yours.

As a parent, you will most likely hire several nannies over the course of your child's growing-up years. How long each nanny stays and what they do will vary as your child grows and your family needs change. They may be called nanny, babysitter, "big sister," travel nanny or au pair. Each will have a unique relationship in part because of who they are and in part because of who you and your child are. Most parents and the nannies they hire value this relationship and appreciate the experience, no matter how short or long.

As a final note, when it's time to say good-bye to your nanny, give yourself and your child the opportunity to reflect on what that relationship meant to each of you in all the positive and negative ways. Developing the capacity to reflect on experiences over time with a caring adult supports resiliency and the ability to overcome adversity and succeed in life.[48] We all want children to have a meaningful life and to succeed in that endeavor. Along this path, relationships are created. One of these is with a nanny, bringing with it all the complexities presented in this book. Outside of the pragmatic support a nanny provides, there exists the individual for who she is and how she is with you and your child. Choosing this individual to be part of your and your child's life at this point in time and nourishing this relationship over time is a gift to be cherished.

---

48   Jack Shonkoff, *The Science of Resilience*, Harvard Graduate School of Education, March 2015.

VOICES FROM YOUNG ADULTS WHO GREW UP WITH A NANNY

· ·

In case the ideas, information and reassurances in this book don't allay worries about outcome, I thought hearing from now-young adults about their experiences with their nanny growing up would add insight! The names are disguised to give privacy but the words are their own. The seven young adults range in age from 14 to 20 years old, all attending either high school or college.

Andrea

Q: Describe your first nanny, Krista, who cared for you for over seven years in 10 words or less:

A: Krista is caring, funny and generally great. One of the nicest people I know. And she's just hilarious too. Just wonderful.

Q: I recall that Krista made life fun for you, something of an adventure?

A: Yes, definitely. I'm really interested in baking and it was primarily Krista who did that. We never bought cookies at the store. She would make them and have me help. It's always great to have chocolate chip cookies. She built on my interest and taught me to do something important.

Q: When you think back, what influence did Krista have in your life?

A: She was always so nice and always thought about other people so that got me thinking about other people instead of myself. Krista is so funny and I know that part of my sense of humor has come from her. It's great to have a very funny role model. She would make jokes and puns and now I just love puns. I have some very funny friends and love joking around with them.

Q: You grew up having a nanny with you from a very young age, so when you think about yourself in the future and when you might have a family of your own, how do you think having had Krista in your life influences what you might choose to do?

A: It was such a good experience for me, like having a second mom or aunt around. It's good to know an adult who isn't your parent. When I was really young, I got to meet all of Krista's friends, meet different people and see new things.

Q: What would you tell a new mom who is starting on this journey?

A: I imagine it's always hard to leave your kid alone with someone you don't really know, but be optimistic and know your kid will learn new things and have new experiences and things will be okay.

Q: Shifting gears to your second nanny, Brigit. She came into your life when you were older. How was it different with Brigit?

A: Because I was older, I needed less of an adventure partner and instead someone to take me to school and be more involved in school. Brigit is more serious (even though she's lots of fun) and very smart, so if I ever have problems at school I can go to her about that. I can talk to her about anything. She's definitely like a big sister or a role model.

Q: What is it that Brigit taught you about having someone like that in your life?

A: Sometimes I get mad about things like everyone does. You don't always want to listen to your parents about stuff like that, telling you to relax or what you should do. But if you have someone else you can talk to and listen to, and trust, it can really help.

Matthew

Q: You and your sister grew up with Krista as your nanny for seven years. Talk about Krista—the kind of person she is and what influence she had on you.

M: Krista's a very happy person, she loves to make jokes, loves to have fun. It's kind of a cliché but she has a childlike joyfulness. I remember her telling me a story about when I was two years old and someone on the radio said "make some f—king noise!" and so she quickly said "make some trucking noise!" so I made some beeping sounds. We laugh about that now.

She has a very positive vibe; she clearly enjoyed being around kids, and around me and my younger sister. She's definitely a positive, happy person and that's rubbed off on me. I like to think of myself as a positive and happy person.

Q: That joke that she made when you were young, do you find yourself making jokes when others might be more serious?

M: There are times I like to make jokes out of situations. Like with the election—I've been having fun with that. It's trying to take a negative situation and make it positive. Krista played a role in my outlook. She and my parents were the three big presences in my life for those first years.

Q: Are there other ways she had an influence on you?

M: I love music. I'm a big hip-hop and rap guy. She didn't think I was listening to the best rap so she gave me CDs of good music. She's still involved in our lives in a big way. We see her every few weeks, hang out with her and her kids, go have fun. Every time I see her, we are so happy.

Q: That sense of joy still holds?

M: Definitely. We make different jokes now that we're older. She wasn't just a nanny, she was a really good friend and still is. She helped me through my first breakup. She was just there for me.

Q: It's nice to be able to lean on someone's shoulder isn't it?

M: Yes, it's times like that when you know who your friends really are.

Q: Any challenges about having a nanny in general?

M: No major ones that I can really think of, except maybe like sixth to eighth grade, I would want to hang out with my friends and not get picked up from school, but in general, I was really lucky. Brigit and Krista were both great. One time at a Giants game we convinced Krista that our parents always let us get cotton candy and we got in such trouble for pulling that. We have a lot of inside jokes with Krista now.

Q: Switching gears to Brigit, tell me a bit about her.

M: She's similar to Krista in some ways—loose and easygoing—but also somewhat stricter. She's not as mischievous. But she's also very relatable and fun to be around. She's a 49ers fan and I am too (but she likes the A's and I like the Giants so she's not perfect). She's not as playful as Krista but very positive to be around. She's someone I can always go to. If you asked me to pick a favorite, I couldn't. They're two different people, they're both great, and I love them both.

Q: What has Brigit taught you about life?

M: She reinforced a lot of what Krista taught me but also taught responsibility and accountability. For example, there were cookies in our pantry, and you can guess what would happen when nobody was looking. She wouldn't get mad if I took the cookies, but she got mad if I lied about it. That was when a lot of those lessons about accountability clicked for me.

Q: What would you want other kids or parents to know about being a kid growing up with a nanny?

M: Let whoever you hire be who they are. Try to hire a fun-loving person, but let them do what they do and be who they are. If they are a good nanny, you won't have to worry about your kids. Don't try and make them your perfect image of a nanny. That only can make things worse.

Robert:

Q: You had a relationship for many years with Maria growing up. What did this relationship teach you about what is important in life?

R: Maria was always to me like a second grandmother and always there for me. She was in my life from the time I was a kid and throughout all my childhood. She took care of me and helped me grow up.

Q: How did your relationship with Maria influence your ideas about parents working while raising kids?

R: It makes it important that you choose someone you trust to take care of your kids and raise them the way you want them to be raised.

Q: Looking back, is there one thing you wish your parents did different?

R: Nothing I can think of.

Q: Anything else you would want parents to know about hiring a nanny?

R: When I was young I didn't like when my parents were gone a lot. I didn't think about how this was going to feel when I was in my 20s. Now, I think it was wonderful to have another person in my life. I really don't think my nanny replaced my parents. She taught me a lot of things about life.

Dave

Q: Your nanny, Sarah, took care of you for almost 11 years from the time you were very young. How would you describe her?

D: Sarah was caring, extremely affectionate, almost like a grandmother rather than a babysitter really. With some babysitters I had, well, I would say they were nice people, but I had a level of affection for Sarah because we had a great relationship. She didn't have a lot and she would give what she had.

Q: When you think back, what influence did she have in your life?

D: I would say she had a huge impact on my life. In terms of values she would teach us right or wrong. We are Christians and went to the Christian school and had the same values. She would teach us different than my parents, but the concept was clear. My parents were clear about what to teach us. With Sarah, she wasn't too hard on us. We had our arguments but they weren't really major. She also turned our whole family into dog lovers. She had a love for animals and she got a dog and I went to training classes. To this day I love animals, and Sarah taught me that.

Q: What would you tell a new mom who is starting on this journey?

D: I would say look for someone who would care for your kids as you would. Also get someone who can stay around for a while. I know a lot of kids that had a lot of different nannies. I think it would suck if that happened to me.

Q: Any challenges about having a nanny in general?

D: It was kind of sad not to see my parents.

Q: What would you want other kids or parents to know about what its like being a kid growing up with a nanny?

D: It's not bad. You're going to end up liking her and it'll be cool and refreshing. She'll be an important person in your life. I honestly can say the main thing is that my life would have been different without her. There would be a piece missing and now it's something I couldn't imagine my life without. It's a really cool relationship to have. I still call her every week. She's an important person in my life.

Susie

Q: Your nanny, Marian, was a live-in nanny and took care of you for almost 17 years, from the time you were very young. How would you describe her?

S: I believe she is an incredible and hard-driven person and truly inspires me. First of all, she was working a lot with other families and anytime I went downstairs to say hello, I saw she had books out, nursing books, and she was always studying

Q: When you think back, what influence did she have in your life?

S: Of all things, she was always in our home because she lived in the room downstairs. So I could hear the garage doors close and knew she was home. Even though she had her own space, she was always there. And to have someone in your life who is always there for you, this is something I value. I now live in the same room she lived in and realize

I can hear everything that goes on upstairs. Everytime my parents and i would argue, she never said anything. She was always there, knew what was going on but she respected our privacy. I really value that.

Q: What would you tell a new mom who is starting on this journey?

S: I personally wouldn't be able to understand what it is like because I was so young when my parents hired Marian. But I would say the initial introduction is important. It's kind of a "gut" thing and trusting your gut. This is something I learned from my parents: look at someone in the eye and if there's anything that seems off then don't do it. Decide if someone wants to really care for the child and if you're getting a feeling like they would truly care.

Q: Any challenges about having a nanny in general?

S: I feel if the nanny is more present than the parents that might pose a problem. I don't know, I never really saw a downside . . . well, until I became a teenager and then I didn't want a nanny! But it was always nice to know she was there for me. She was always extremely respectful and kept to herself when she needed to. One time I didn't tell her I was coming home and when she heard me upstairs, she came up to make sure it was me. She didn't say anything to make me feel I did something wrong. She just said, "I heard someone come in and wanted to be sure it was you."

Q: What would you want other kids or parents to know about being a kid growing up with a nanny?

S: It's just another adult you can trust. I trusted Marian a lot. She knew some things my parents didn't know. Especially if you've grown up with them, they've seen you grow and know who you are and don't judge you. There's someone who is going to be there for you – a trusting adult. She became like a best friend to me.

Q: Other comments?

S: I cried when she left . . . She didn't know that. We didn't formally say goodbye. It was hard for both of us. We said our good-byes though. She'll always be part of my life especially since she's been in my life since I was a baby.

Mary and Tom

Q: When you think back on having Trisha as your nanny full-time for the first eight years of your life, what influence did she have on your life?

M: She has been a positive influence in my life. I still get texts from her and we still talk often. She's another adult figure I can trust. The values she taught me are how to be responsible, while kicking and screaming sometimes! She taught me to be adventurous. It was all very positive.

T: To me, it's like having an extra parent or grandparent. I can trust her, and we still get presents for every Hanukah or birthday.

Q: Any challenges about having a nanny in general?

M: None that I can think of.

T: Maybe I was a little less independent, having someone doing a lot for me when I was younger. It's not a big deal but having someone there when you need them is great, but then it means you don't get to do as much for yourself.

Q: What would you tell a new mom who is starting on this journey?

M: Don't worry, your kids will be in capable hands.

T: It might be hard or scary to put your child in the hands of someone you don't particularly know very well, but they are capable, qualified, caring people and it will be, for the most part, a positive influence.

Q: What would you want other kids to know about what it's like to grow up with a nanny?

M: It's kind of like having another family member, like another aunt or grandparent who cares for you. My aunts and uncles live very far away, so I was closer to Trisha and she was like another aunt.

T: I don't really agree with what Mary just said. I think it's a nice alternative to having a family member living near us. I can't say I'm closer to Trisha than them. I would tell a kid not to worry about it too much. But, I really don't remember a time when I didn't have a nanny, so I can't say I know what to say to someone who didn't have one.

CONCLUSION

I hope this book has given you some insight into the complexities, joys, wonder and satisfaction of hiring a nanny for your child and your family. Embarking on a journey to be the best parent you can be presents opportunities laden with unanticipated challenges. One of these is childcare. Do you want and need childcare assistance as part of your parenting journey; and if so, is hiring a nanny the right choice? I hope the information in these pages has provided an appreciation for what it can be like to include a nanny in your family life.

I hope this book has provided you with a road map, direction and tools to keep you on track throughout the hiring process. Hiring a nanny is such an important decision! You will need navigation to direct your journey, ensuring you are headed where you want to go and that the finish line is in sight. Many parents have gone through this process successfully, and I hope you have gained insight and some camaraderie from their stories.

Finally, I hope the book imparts a central message that relationships matter. The quality and type of relationship you create with your nanny has an impact on the quality of the relationship your nanny has with your child. Act intentionally and choose wisely. Reflect on the experience and enjoy this special time in your life!

CHECKLISTS AND FORMS

JOB BASICS

Job Title	Nanny Arrangement	Documentations
Nanny	Live Out	Department of Homeland Security
Mother's Helper	Live-In	Internal Revenue Service
Family Assistant	Share Care	DMV (driver's license/ID)
Au-Pair	Co-op	Workers Compensation
Doula	Staffed Household	
Housecleaner		
Babysitter	**Schedule**	**Compensation**
Special Needs Therapist	Full Time	Salary Range_____ Wk/Mo/Yr
Tutor	Part Time	Taxable Income
	Flexible Hours/Days	
	Travel	Benefits
	Overnight Care	
		Vacation
		Holidays
		Sick Pay
		Medical Insurance Premiums
		Retirement IRA Contribution
		Room and Board
		Cell Phone
		Nanny Car for personal use

RESPONSIBILITIES

Childcare	Housework	Errands
Feeding	Child's room kept clean	Grocery shopping, as needed
Changing	Toys clean and put away	Dry cleaning
Bathing	Bed linens clean/put away	Post Office or FedEx/UPS
Providing Safe Care	Child's laundry	
Plan daily activities	Family laundry	Pet Care
Maintains daily journal	Family meal preparation	
Child meal preparation	Cleans up after herself	Feeding pet(s)
Tutoring	Straightens up main areas	
Transporting child		
Collaboration with professionals		

REQUIREMENTS		
Education/Training	**Childcare Experience**	**Languages**
Early Childhood Education	Infant/toddler	English
State teaching credential	Preschool	Spanish
Special needs certification	Elementary	French
Continued education	Adolescent	German
Workshops	Group care Multiples	Chinese-Mandarin
		Chinese-Cantonese
		Other
Health Safety Requirements	**Background Check**	
CPR/First Aid training	Criminal in all counties resided	
TB test clearance	Social Security verification	
TiDaP and MMR vaccination	Driving record	
Flu shot	Civil Protective orders	

EMPLOYER-EMPLOYEE DOCUMENTS	
Employee Requirements	**Employer Requirements**
Resume	Worker's Compensation
References	Auto insurance for nanny
Photo	Authorization to drive form
Certificates of education/training	Emergency medical treatment form
CPR/first aid certificate	Important phone numbers
TB test clearance	Disaster plan
Driving license	
Driving record	
Criminal and civil background check	
Social security verification	
IRS W-4	
DHS I-9	
Contract	

JOB ANNOUNCEMENT: SAMPLE

INFANT-TODDLER NANNY FOR BUSY FAMILY

We are first-time parents and need an experienced, knowledgeable, maternal and family-oriented nanny to join us in raising our now 3-month-old daughter while supporting our family over the long term! The schedule is Monday – Friday, 8 – 6 p.m., with the flexibility to work additional hours as needed.

We have busy work schedules and need our nanny to be fully in charge while in close communication with us during the day. We respect the value of education/training as well as hands-on experience caring for infants/toddlers. We hope to find this combination in our nanny. Our home is close to shops, libraries, parks and public transportation.

REQUIREMENTS

The primary responsibility is creating a responsible, loving relationship with our daughter in partnership with us while ensuring all aspects of our daughter's care is met and her daily routines and activities run smoothly.

- Many years of experience as a nanny, teacher or a parent caring for infants and toddlers
- Loving, kind, nurturing, maternal and patient personality
- Physically fit, high energy and happy demeanor
- Conscientious: diligent about maintaining routine, sending texts to parents
- English language fluency (2nd language a plus!)
- Legal immigration status
- Amenable to tax withholding
- Clear background checks, etc.
- Strong references
- Willingness to help with light housekeeping, laundry, organization and other projects during hours when children are sleeping
- Driver's license and clean driving record

IDEAL CHARACTERISTICS AND SKILLS

A high importance is placed on honesty, integrity, understanding of children's development and idiosyncrasies, communication, organization, professionalism, warmth and experience. Other characteristics:

- Engaged and attentive with children
- Educated
- Playful with lots of stamina
- Has a good sense of humor
- Resourceful
- Takes initiative and follows through

SCHEDULE

Monday – Friday, 8 a.m. – 6 p.m.
Flexibility to work evenings/weekends as needed.

COMPENSATION AND BENEFITS

A professional taxable salary, including benefits, will be provided.

CONTACT

INTERVIEW QUESTIONS: SAMPLE

Some questions you can ask of candidates to evaluate their **experience with children** are:

1. Can you tell me about the children you have cared for? What were their personalities like? How did you get to know them?

2. Among the children you have cared for, who was the most challenging? What was it about this child that was particularly challenging for you?

3. What do you expect a newborn to be learning about his or her world? What about a five-month-old?

4. How do you help children keep predictable routines of eating, sleeping, playing, etc.? What has been your experience with different children doing this? What has been your experience with different families?

5. If you had a child-rearing philosophy that best defines your way of understanding and caring for a child, what would that be?

6. Our son is always on the go and loves to interact! He's curious about the world and asks tons of questions. Can you talk about a child you have cared for that has a similar temperament and view of the world? How did you spend your days together?

7. Discipline—or setting reasonable limits—is important for our family. What are some ways to help preschool children learn to know what these are, and how do you handle those situations when our son doesn't want to do what is expected?

8. Imagine you are home alone with our baby all day. It's raining and impossible to go outside. How would you spend your time with her?

9. Imagine you are home alone with our daughter in the evening. It's raining. Suddenly you hear a loud banging on the front door. A man yells to you that he has had an accident and is badly hurt. He wants to use the phone and call someone to help him. What would you do?

10. Imagine you are home alone with our daughter. She is eating her snack and suddenly chokes on her food. What would you do?

11. Imagine you are driving our child to pick up groceries at the store. It's cold and rainy. Our child is sleeping in the backseat. What would you do?

Some questions you can ask of candidates to evaluate their **personality and character** are:

1. Why do you want to work as a nanny?

2. Look forward five years . . . Someone is talking about you! What would you want the person to say about you and what you are doing?

3. What activities have meaning for you?

4. What do you feel passionate about? What makes you happy?

5. When are you unable to laugh at yourself?

6. How would you describe your style when you care for children?

7. If you trusted us enough as your employer to know how to manage you most effectively, what tips would you give us about how you are best managed?

Some questions you can ask of candidates to evaluate their **family and personal values** are:

1. Can you tell me one piece of advice that was handed down to you by your parents that reflects a value important to you?

2. We all learn from the culture we grew up in what is important in life. How is it different growing up in your culture than here in the U.S.?

Some questions you can ask of candidates to evaluate your **potential employer/employee relationship** are:

1. In many nannies' working relationship with parents, there are inevitably difficult situations that come up that can be hard to talk about. Can you tell me about those you have experienced? How did you talk about them and how were they resolved?

2. What should we know about you to make sure you are comfortable in our home? Please tell us what special requests you have. For example, do you have any dietary restrictions; are there religious holidays you want to observe; do you have vacation or travel plans? How would you be certain to have your privacy when you need it?

THE INSTITUTE for FAMILIES and NANNIES

LEARN TOGETHER.
CARE TOGETHER.

NANNY CANDIDATE EVALUATION FORM

Personal Characteristics										
Warm, nurturing	1	2	3	4	5	6	7	8	9	10
Trustworthy	1	2	3	4	5	6	7	8	9	10
Really loves children	1	2	3	4	5	6	7	8	9	10
Shares ideas	1	2	3	4	5	6	7	8	9	10
Strong work ethic	1	2	3	4	5	6	7	8	9	10
Trustworthy	1	2	3	4	5	6	7	8	9	10
Mature	1	2	3	4	5	6	7	8	9	10
Good judgment	1	2	3	4	5	6	7	8	9	10
Good sense of humor	1	2	3	4	5	6	7	8	9	10
Bright and smart	1	2	3	4	5	6	7	8	9	10
Calm	1	2	3	4	5	6	7	8	9	10
Direct	1	2	3	4	5	6	7	8	9	10
Punctual and reliable	1	2	3	4	5	6	7	8	9	10
Flexible	1	2	3	4	5	6	7	8	9	10
Respects privacy	1	2	3	4	5	6	7	8	9	10
Communication										
Open and direct	1	2	3	4	5	6	7	8	9	10
Easy to understand	1	2	3	4	5	6	7	8	9	10
Easy to be with	1	2	3	4	5	6	7	8	9	10
Verbal	1	2	3	4	5	6	7	8	9	10
Childcare Orientations and Skills										
Experienced	1	2	3	4	5	6	7	8	9	10
Knows development	1	2	3	4	5	6	7	8	9	10
Recognizes differences	1	2	3	4	5	6	7	8	9	10

Knowledgeable	1	2	3	4	5	6	7	8	9	10
Creative	1	2	3	4	5	6	7	8	9	10
Knows community	1	2	3	4	5	6	7	8	9	10
Capable	1	2	3	4	5	6	7	8	9	10
Knows nutrition	1	2	3	4	5	6	7	8	9	10
Household Assistance										
Clean and neat	1	2	3	4	5	6	7	8	9	10
Organized	1	2	3	4	5	6	7	8	9	10
Takes initiative	1	2	3	4	5	6	7	8	9	10
Ethics										
Honest	1	2	3	4	5	6	7	8	9	10
Respectful	1	2	3	4	5	6	7	8	9	10
Integrity	1	2	3	4	5	6	7	8	9	10

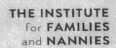

SAMPLE NANNY CONTRACT

DATE: _____

Re: Employment Agreement

Dear Nanny:

We are very pleased that you have agreed to work for us as a professional nanny for our daughter. This letter, including the attached "Terms of Employment," is your Employment Agreement.

Terms of Employment

Starting _____, 2017 we will employ you to work as our nanny.

The attached "Terms of Employment" sets out the terms of your employment. If these terms are acceptable to you, please sign below and return the signed letter to us.

We look forward to working with you.

Very truly yours,

_____

* * * * *

I agree to the terms of my employment set out in the attached "Terms of Employment."

TERMS OF EMPLOYMENT

Nanny:	
Parents:	
Position:	Live-out nanny for Parents' Child(ren).
Pre-Employ-ment Criteria	a. Criminal Background Check clearance b. National Sex Offenders Registry clearance c. TB Test results with a negative finding d. CPR / First Aid training certificate e. TiDaP and MMR vaccination f. Social Security Verification g. Valid Driver's License h. Department of Motor Vehicles Record I. Personal / Professional references j. Signed Employment Agreement
Start Date:	Nanny will commence work on _____, 2017.
General Duties:	Nanny will provide childcare for Child(ren) and will: • Provide exceptional care for Employers' children • Assist Employer in other activities necessary to maintain a structured and organized household
Daily Care of Child(ren):	Nanny's daily activities include: • Feeding, bathing, changing Child(ren) • Plan, prepare and take Child(ren) for daily walks or other age-appropriate, educational and/or play-based activities. • Maintain a regular schedule approved by Parents for feeding/meals, naps and activities. • Prepare healthy meals and snacks for Child(ren). Feed Child(ren). Clean up after meals. • Play with Child(ren) at home and outdoors. Read books, talk and sing to Child(ren). Teach Child(ren) in age-appropriate ways to support development. • Teach Child(ren) values of respecting others, their place and things, manners, differences among others and getting along with others. • If Parents request, give Child(ren) a bath. • Tell Parents if we need to buy any food, supplies, toys or anything else for Child(ren). • Communicate with Parents about Child(ren), including health, problems, well-being and discipline.

Other Duties:	Nanny's other duties include: • Pick up and organize toys and books. • Keep Child(ren)'s rooms, toys and other personal items clean. • Wash, dry, fold and put away Child(ren)'s laundry • Prepare meals for Child(ren) • Clean up after meals • Perform errands for the household if possible • Assist during emergencies and other unusual circumstances.
House Rules:	Nanny agrees to abide by all "house rules" during working hours, including but not limited to the following: • No visitors at the house, unless Parents have approved. • No smoking, drinking or drug use. • Do not open the door to anyone unless the person identifies him/herself and Parents have given Nanny prior notice and approval of his/her admittance to the house. • Limit personal phone calls to what is absolutely necessary. • In case of emergency, call Parents at _____ (mom) or _____ (dad) or grandmother at _____ or friend _____ or, if true emergency, 911. • No television for Child(ren). • No physical discipline or yelling. • Nanny must be available to Parents by cell phone at all times. • Contact Parents immediately about any problems with the house.

| Health and Safety of Child(ren): | Nanny agrees to abide by the following health and safety rules when caring for the Child(ren):
• Do not leave Child(ren) unattended at any time. Do not leave Child(ren) with any other person.
• Remove any toys that are broken or unsafe.
• Do not feed Child(ren) sugary or unhealthy foods such as juice, cookies, cake, cupcakes, candy, croissants, etc. Child(ren) should eat healthy foods such as fruits, vegetables, cheese, yoghurt, oatmeal, meat, tofu, fish, beans, etc. Child(ren) should only drink water and milk.
• Do not take Child(ren) in any car, taxi or bus unless Parents have given prior approval.
• Use of car seats for Child(ren) and seat belts for adults is required at all times.
• Do not eat, drink or use cell phone unless on Bluetooth while driving Child(ren).
• Keep Child(ren) away from dogs and other animals unless you have determined that the dog is safe and owner of dog confirms that dog is safe.
• Contact Parents immediately about any problems with Child(ren), such as sickness or injury.
• Wash hands upon arriving at house each day, after using the restroom and whenever they are dirty.
• Wash Child(ren)'s hands before and after meals, and whenever they are dirty.
• Keep Child(ren) away from painted surfaces, peeling paint and paint chips.
• Do not give Child(ren) any medicine unless Parents request. If you administer medication, you must record the time, date and the dosage administered.
• Nanny must carry "Emergency Medical Treatment Authorization" for Child(ren) at all times and know where to locate the copy in the home.
• At Parents' expense, Nanny will take an annual re-certification Infant/Child(ren) CPR/First Aid training course at a location approved by Parents.
• Nanny will be familiar with the location, use and operation of all emergency equipment at Parents' residence.
• Nanny will be familiar with Parents' emergency procedures, such as medical, fire and disaster preparedness and carry out these procedures in a timely, efficient manner when necessary.
• Notify Parents immediately in the event that Nanny is sick or injured in any way.
• Provide to Parents the name, address and telephone number of two relatives/friends to contact in the event of an emergency. |
| Hours: | Nanny will work the following schedule to include as needed evenings and weekdays as may be requested by Parents and agreed by Nanny.
Monday – Friday 8:00 am – 6:00 pm |

Pay:	Parents will pay Nanny $_____ per hour for all hours worked less than 8 hours per day and 40 hours weekly. Parents will pay Nanny $_____ overtime for all hours worked greater than 40 hours weekly or over 8 hours per day. Should Nanny provide overnight care, Nanny will be paid at her regular hourly rate until 9:00 p.m. and after 6:00 a.m. During the hours from 9:00 p.m. and 6:00 a.m., Nanny will be paid an "on-call" rate adjusted to current minimum wage. Should the Child(ren) require care during the night, Nanny will be paid at her regular hourly rate, including the applicable overtime rate.
Sick Days:	After 90 days' employment, Employee will earn one hour of sick leave for every 30 hours worked, accrued up to a maximum of 24 hours for part-time employment and 40 hours for full-time employment during the time of employment. Accrued sick leave can be used to care for Employee's family member(s) or relative(s). Unused sick leave is not paid out at the time employment terminates.
Car:	Nanny will have use of a designated car of Parents as needed to carry out her duties.
Confidentiality:	Nanny agrees that all personal, family or other information with respect to Parents and/or their family, friends and associates is confidential. Nanny will keep such information confidential and will not disclose it to anyone at any time, unless Parents have given prior written consent. This obligation will continue to apply even after Nanny's position with Parents has ended.
At-Will Employment:	Nanny's employment is solely on an at will basis, terminable by either Nanny or Parents for any reason at any time, with or without cause. Nothing in this Employment Agreement, or in the prior or subsequent course of conduct between the parties, shall be construed to create a contract for a term of years, a contract terminable only for good cause, or any relationship between the parties other than one of at will employment.
Termination of Employment:	Nanny is free to leave her job and terminate this Employment Agreement at any time for any reason. Similarly, Parents are free to end Nanny's employment and terminate this Employment Agreement at any time for any reason. If either party does so terminate following the first 90 days of employment (the Probationary Period), a 30-day notice will be given. Parents will pay Nanny any earned but unpaid wages (subject to withholding for any applicable federal or state taxes) and the parties will return to each other any personal property of the other.
Other Legal Provisions:	This Employment Agreement contains the entire agreement between Nanny and Parents regarding Nanny's employment and supersedes any other agreements, representations, promises, or understandings, whether oral, written or implied, alleged to exist. No agreement, promise or representation not contained in this Agreement shall be binding on either party. This Employment Agreement is entered into in the State of California, and shall be governed by and construed in accordance with California law.

EMERGENCY PROCEDURES: EMPLOYER LIST

Create a Home File and place all completed forms in this file in a prominent location for easy access by Nanny, Babysitters, Visitors and Parents to use as needed.

1. Complete the Important Telephone Numbers Form
   a. Copy goes to nanny

2. Complete the Emergency Medical Treatment Form for your child
   a. Copies go to nanny's wallet, in child(ren)'s diaper bag, in nanny's car, in parent's car, in the child(ren)'s files in the pediatrician's office.

3. Complete the Authorization to Drive Form
   a. Copy goes to nanny's car and your car

4. Review Evacuation Procedures in the event of a fire
   a. Purchase Fire Escape Ladder and place in location near upper-level window or deck
   b. Place BabyBjörn near the escape ladder to carry child(ren) safely down
   c. Purchase fire extinguisher for kitchen and garage
   d. Review procedure with nanny to remove and use extinguisher(s) in each location

5. Review Burglar and Fire Alarm System with Nanny, including security code needed to verify alarm when responder calls.

6. Create Disaster Plan and Review Procedure with Nanny

a. From your mobile phone, download the app directly from the app link and search for "red cross." Download the Earthquake Notification app - or contact the Red Cross and they will send you a link to download the quake alert app to your iPhone or Android device, or you can download them directly from the iTunes or Google Play app stores.

b. Designate an Out-of-State Person as Coordinator to contact during an emergency

c. Determine two locations (1) near your home and (2) outside the neighborhood within walking distance where everyone will meet if it is unsafe to stay in the home or the neighborhood is evacuated.

d. Purchase a backpack for the children and place items needed to keep the child(ren) warm, fed and medically safe for 2 to 3 days (e.g. clothing, food, water, emergency treatment form, medical supplies, whistle, neon blanket, cell phone battery, cash, etc.)

FOUR ESSENTIAL HEALTH AND SAFETY ISSUES

There are several health and safety issues you want to discuss with your nanny.

1. Medical emergencies

2. Earthquake and Flood Preparedness

3. Fire fighting

4. Police

Medical Emergencies

Before leaving your child with your nanny for the first time, be certain you have posted a list of names and contact numbers of people who can be reached in a medical emergency. Don't put the list in a drawer or on a cluttered bulletin board! Your nanny may not find it when she needs it.

There are three levels of medical emergencies that can occur with children. Review these with your nanny and provide her with the important information and paperwork to handle them.

Level I: The Expectable Bumps and Bruises of Daily Life

Children fall, bump their head or scratch their knees. Nannies should treat the injury and contact the parents when they return home.

- Nannies should know where to locate the first aid supplies in the home and car.

Level II: Child's Health Requires Immediate Attention

Children can injure themselves, suddenly spike a fever or otherwise require immediate medical attention. Nannies should contact the parents immediately and together decide a course of action. This may require an emergency visit to the pediatrician, after-hours clinic or hospital.

- Nannies should carry an Emergency Medical Treatment Form in their purse and car and know where to locate one in the home. This form contains all the information medical personnel need to begin treatment without waiting for the parents to show up.

- Nannies should know where the pediatrician's office, after-hours clinic and hospital emergency room are located. The nanny's name should be in the child's medical record file so she is known to be the child's caregiver.

Level III: 911 Call

Nannies should recognize when a 911 call is required and what information to provide when making the call. Nannies should call 911 first and then contact the parents.

- Information to give 911 operator
    a. Address (House Number, Street, City and Cross Street)
    b. Telephone number (including area code)
    c. Number of people injured
    d. Names of the children injured
    e. Ages of the children injured
    f. Nature of the emergency (burn, broken bone, can't breathe, choking, heart stopped)

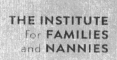

Disaster Preparedness

Review with your nanny the procedures for handling disasters. Show her the location of the Emergency Disaster Kit and where you will all meet if it is not safe to be in your home. A disaster kit should be located near the safest exit of your home and an additional kit should be kept in the car.

- Nannies should have contact information for two responsible adults who live out of state and who would be notified of the nanny and child's location when a disaster occurs. Cell phones for local calls are not reliable in a disaster.

Fire Safety

Review the location of and how to use the fire extinguishers and smoke detectors in your home. A Nanny should also know the best escape routes from your home in a fire and how to find them if there is thick smoke.

Police Safety

If you have a burglar alarm system in your home, review the procedures to activate/deactivate the alarm, including the code to provide the response unit when an alarm is sounded so they know it is a valid call.

IMPORTANT TELEPHONE NUMBERS

MOTHER   (W) _____   (Cell) _____

FATHER   (W) _____   (Cell) _____

GRANDPARENTS   _____   _____

                (H) _____   (Cell) _____

PEDIATRICIAN   _____   Tel: _____

URGENT CARE   _____

POISON CONTROL _____

EMERGENCIES   _____**911**_____

FIRE (non-emergency) _____

POLICE (non-emergency) _____

TAXI / UBER _____

THE INSTITUTE
for **FAMILIES**
and **NANNIES**

LEARN TOGETHER.
CARE TOGETHER.

EMERGENCIES

In a life-threatening emergency, immediately call 911 for all emergency services (medical, police, or fire). When calling 911, you will be talking with an emergency dispatcher. The dispatcher will ask questions to determine your location and the type of emergency services you need.

Dial 911.

1. **Tell the person who answers:**
   a. Address "We are at _____
      in _____
   b. The cross street is _____ _____
   c. My telephone number here is _____ _____ (including area code).
   d. Number of people injured
   e. Names of the children injured
   f. Ages of the children injured
   g. Nature of the emergency (burn, broken bone, can't breathe, choking, heart stopped)

2. **Stay on the line.**

Many dispatchers are trained to give instructions before emergency services arrive. They can assist you with certain life-saving techniques, such as CPR or rescue breathing. Therefore, do not hang up until the dispatcher tells you it is OK to do so.

FIRE SAFETY

Fire Department (non-emergency): _____

Fire Extinguisher Location: _____

Fire Alarm Location: _____

Escape Routes from the House _____

Location to meet if house is unsafe: _____

Natural Disasters

Emergency Disaster Kit location: _____

Emergency Kit last updated on: _____

(Batteries checked, food within expiration date, supplies sufficient for current family size/special needs)

In the Event of an Earthquake or Mud Slide, follow the Family Disaster Plan

_____

AUTHORIZATION TO TREAT A MINOR

This consent shall remain effective until _____, 20__.

I (we) the undersigned parent, parents or legal guardian of _____, a minor, do hereby authorize and consent to any x-ray examination, anesthetic, medical or surgical diagnosis rendered under the general or special supervision of any member of the medical staff and emergency room staff licensed under the provisions of the Medicine Practice Act, or a Dentist licensed under the provisions of the Dental Practice Act, and on the staff of any acute general hospital holding a current license to operate a hospital from the state of California Department of Public Health. It is understood that this authorization is given in advance of any specific diagnosis, treatment or hospital care being required but is given to provide authority and power to render care which the aforementioned physician in the exercise of his best judgment may deem advisable. It is understood that effort shall be made to contact the undersigned prior to rendering treatment to the patient, but that any of the above treatment will not be withheld if the undersigned cannot be reached.

Date of Birth: _____

List any restrictions: _____

Last Tetanus Toxoid Booster: _____ _____

List Vaccinations Received: _____ _____

Allergies to Drugs or Foods: _____ _____

Any Special Medications or Pertinent Information: _____

Parent/Guardian Name: _____

Contact Numbers: (W) _____ (H) _____

(C) _____

Parent/Guardian Name: _____

Contact Numbers: (W) _____ (H) _____ (C) _____

Pediatrician's Name: _____ Tel: _____

Address: _____ City: _____ State _____ Zip: _____

Insurance Company: _____ Policy No.: _____

Signature of Parent(s) or Legal Guardian: _____ Date: _____

Address: _____ City: _____ State _____

THE INSTITUTE
for **FAMILIES**
and **NANNIES**

LEARN TOGETHER.
CARE TOGETHER.

DRIVER AUTHORIZATION

I hereby authorize _____ to drive my

child(ren), _____.

Nanny may be driving the following automobile(s):

Model: _____

Year: _____

Color: _____

License Plate Number: _____

Model: _____

Year: _____

Color: _____

License Plate Number: _____

Nanny's Driver's License Number: _____

Parent's Name _____

Telephone Number _____

_____   _____

Parent's Signature   Date

DISASTER PREPAREDNESS KIT

**Remember: Determine the location to meet if unsafe to stay in the home**

Earthquake Notification App by Red Cross

Be ready for an earthquake with Earthquake by American Red Cross. Receive alerts and notifications when an earthquake occurs, prepare your family and home, find help and let others know you are safe even if the power is out – a must have for anyone who lives in an earthquake-prone area or has loved ones who do. From your mobile phone, download the APP directly from the APP link and search for "redcross".

Disaster preparedness kit items should be stored in a portable, durable, waterproof container(s) near, or as close as possible to, the exit door. Review the contents of your kit at least once per year or as your family needs change.

FAMILY DISASTER PLAN[49]

Meet with your family and discuss why you need to prepare for disaster. Explain the dangers of fire, severe weather and earthquakes to children. Plan to share responsibilities nad work together as a team.

Discuss the types of disasters that are most likely to happen. Explain what to do in each case.

Make sure everyone knows where to find your disaster supply kit and Go kits (Go-kits are emergency kits you pack in advance so that if an emergency strikes, you just pick up the kit and GO!)

1. Have a flashlight, a pair of shoes and clothes in a plastic bag under everyone's bed in case there is an earthquake during the night.

2. Determine the best escape routes from your home. Try and identify two escape routes.

3. Pick two places to meet:
   a. Right outside your home in case of a sudden emergency, like a fire
   b. Outside your neighborhood in case you can't return home. Everyone must know the address and your contact's phone number

4. Discuss what to do in an evacuation

5. Plan how to take care of your pets.

---

49 San Francisco NERT Training Materials, San Francisco, CA 2017

6. Practice your evacuation routes: Duck, Cover and Hold, and Stop Drop and Roll drills

7. Create emergency response cards for each of your family members

8. Next, find out about the disaster plans at your workplace, your children's school or daycare center and other places where your family spends time.

9. Make copies of important documents and inventory valuables. Keep these in a safe deposit box or with someone outside of the immediate area.

Family Disaster Contact Plan: After a disaster, each person should call the designated contact person to report his/her location and condition. This person should be out-of-state because it is often easier to call long distance after a disaster.

Designated Out-of-State Contact Person:

_____

Phone: _____

GLOSSARY

au-pair: A non-U.S.-born woman between the ages of 18 and 26 years who immigrates to the U.S. on a U.S. Government-issued visa to provide up to 40 hours per week of childcare in return for a small stipend, room/board and the cultural experience of living with an American family for one year, with the option to extend to two years.

Authorization to Drive: A form completed by both parent and nanny that gives a nanny authorization to drive the parent's children in the parent's or nanny's car.

California Child Abuse Index: Database of child abuse investigations maintained by the California Attorney General's Child Protection Program.

California Department of Justice (DOJ): The department mandated to maintain the statewide criminal record repository for the State of California. The DOJ is authorized by California statute to process State of California and Federal Bureau of Investigation (FBI) fingerprint-based background checks.

California Identification Card: Photo identification dispensed by the California Department of Motor Vehicles.

CPR: Cardio Pulmonary Resuscitation.

DCAP: Dependent Care Assistance Plan, a flexible spending account an employer sets up that allows employees to pay dependent care expenses with pre-tax dollars. The employer also receives tax benefits. Employees may set aside up to $5,000 of their salaries in salaries to pay for dependent care.

Department of Homeland Security (DHS): The federal agency responsible for leading a unified national effort to secure and protect the United States of America against terrorist attacks, threats and other hazards to the nation.

Department of Homeland Security and Immigration Reform and Control Act: Public Law 99-603 (Act of 11/6/86), which was passed in order to control and deter illegal immigration to the United States. Its major provisions stipulate legalization of undocumented aliens who had been continuously unlawfully present since 1982, legalization of certain agricultural workers, sanctions for employers who knowingly hire undocumented workers and increased enforcement at U.S. borders.

Department of Labor: A cabinet-level department of the U.S. federal government responsible for occupational safety, wage and hour standards, unemployment insurance benefits, reemployment services, and some economic statistics; many U.S. states also have such departments.

Department of Motor Vehicles: The state agency that registers motor vehicles and boats and issues driver's licenses in the U.S. state of California. It regulates new car dealers, commercial cargo carriers, private driving schools and private traffic schools. The DMV works with the Superior Courts of California to promptly record convictions against driver's licenses and subsequently suspends or revokes licenses when a driver accumulates too many convictions. It issues California license plates and driver's licenses. The DMV also issues identification cards to people who are ineligible for, or do not wish to have, a driver's license.

Domestic Worker: A person who works within the employer's household. Domestic workers perform a variety of household services for an individual or a family, from providing care for children and elderly dependents to housekeeping, including cleaning and household maintenance.

Domestic Workers' Bill of Rights: A Domestic Workers' Bill of Rights took effect in New York State on November 29, 2010. Among other rights, this law gave domestic workers the right to overtime pay, a day of rest every seven days, three paid days of rest each year (after one year of work for the same employer), protection under the state human rights law, and a special cause of action for domestic workers who suffer sexual or racial harassment. In July 2013, Hawaii became the second state to implement basic labor protections for domestic workers. In January 2014, similar legislation took effect in California.

doula: a birth companion and post-birth supporter, is a nonmedical person who assists a woman before, during, and/or after childbirth, as well as her spouse and/or family, by providing physical assistance and emotional support.

DUI: Driving under the influence, the act of operating a motor vehicle after having consumed alcohol (ethanol) or other drugs, to the degree that mental and motor skills are impaired.

EEOC: Equal Employment Opportunity Commission, a federal agency that administers and enforces civil rights laws against workplace discrimination. The EEOC investigates discrimination complaints based on an individual's race, children, national origin, religion, sex, age, disability, gender identity or genetic information, and retaliation for reporting, participating in, and/or opposing a discriminatory practice.

FICA: A United States federal payroll (or employment) tax imposed on both employees and employers to fund Social Security and Medicare—federal programs that provide benefits for retirees, disabled people, and children of deceased workers.

first aid: Medical techniques that an individual, either with or without formal medical training, can be trained to perform with minimal equipment.

gross salary: The agreed/committed compensation to be paid on a periodic basis against services for that period. Gross salary is generally considered to be compensation before taxes are withheld.

I-9: A United States Citizenship and Immigration Services form. Mandated by the Immigration Reform and Control Act of 1986, it is used to verify the identity and legal authorization to work of all paid employees in the United States.

Immigration Reform and Control Act (IRCA): *See* Department of Homeland Security and Immigration Reform and Control Act.

independent contractor: An individual or entity that provides goods or services on an "as needed" basis.

International Nanny Association (INA): The umbrella association for the in-home childcare industry by providing information, education and guidance to the public and to industry professionals.

IRS: The revenue service of the United States federal government. The government agency is a bureau of the Department of the Treasury, and is under the immediate direction of the Commissioner of Internal Revenue, who is appointed for a five-year term by the President of the United States. The IRS is responsible for collecting taxes and administering the Internal Revenue Code, the federal statutory tax law of the U.S. Its duty to maximize tax revenue entails providing tax assistance to taxpayers, as well as pursuing and resolving instances of erroneous or fraudulent tax filings. The IRS has also overseen various benefits programs and enforces portions of the Affordable Care Act.

LGBT: Acronym that relates to the diversity of the lesbian/gay/bisexual/transgender culture.

livable wage: The living wage differs from the minimum wage in that the latter is set by law and can fail to meet the requirements to have a basic quality of life and leaves the family to rely on government programs for additional income.

market rate: The going rate for goods or services is the usual price charged for them in a free **market**. If demand goes up, manufacturers and laborers will tend to respond by increasing the price they require, thus setting a higher market rate.

Mary Poppins: A fictional character first created by P. L. Travers and often viewed as the ideal nanny.

Medicare taxes: The payroll tax that applies to all earned income and supports your health coverage when you become eligible for Medicare. The tax is automatically deducted from an employee's paycheck each month and is a tax on earnings, including wages, tips, certain Railroad Retirement Tax Act (RRTA) benefits, and self-employment earnings that fall above a certain level. There is no minimum income limit, and all individuals who work in the United States must pay the Medicare tax on their earnings.

minimum wage: The federal minimum wage provisions are contained in the Fair Labor Standards Act (FLSA). The federal minimum wage is $7.25 per hour effective July 24, 2009. Many states also have minimum wage laws. Some state laws provide greater employee protections; employers must comply with both. Nannies are entitled to minimum wage, except for babysitters under the age of 18.

Mrs. Doubtfire: The title character of an Academy Award-winning 1993 comedy film about a warm, middle-aged American nanny.

Newborn Care Specialist: The NCSA is an international association dedicated to the professional Newborn Care Specialist. It has been developed to oversee ongoing education in the field of newborn care.

overtime law: The federal overtime provisions are contained in the Fair Labor Standards Act (FLSA). Unless exempt, employees covered by the Act must receive overtime pay for hours worked over 40 in a workweek at a rate not less than time and one-half their regular rates of pay. There is no limit in the Act on the number of hours employees aged 16 and older may work in any workweek. The Act does not require overtime pay for work on Saturdays, Sundays, holidays, or regular days of rest, unless overtime is worked on such days.

Portfolio: A collection of documents gathered and presented by individuals seeking employment. A nanny portfolio usually consists of a photo, cover letter, résumé, references, medical clearance forms, identification and certificates of achievement.

SAHM: Stay-at-home-mom.

share-care: An arrangement whereby two or more families share a common caregiver.

Social Security: A U.S. social insurance program funded by employee payroll contributions to provide benefits for retirement, disability, survivorship, and death.

special needs child: Usually refers to any child with physical or emotional challenges.

TrustLine Registry: A database of nannies and babysitters that have cleared criminal background checks in California.

Tuberculosis: A highly infectious disease caused by bacteria called *mycebacterium tuberculosis* that attacks the lungs, kidney, spine and brain.

W-2: Form W-2, Wage and Tax Statement, is used in the United States income tax system as an information return to report wages paid to employees and the taxes withheld from them.

W-4: Employee's Withholding Allowance Certification Form, completed by an employee so the employer can withhold the correct amount of federal income tax from pay.

~~~~~~~~~~

Clinton, Hillary Rodham. *It Takes a Village*. New York: Simon & Schuster, 1996.

Chase, Stella and Alexander Thomas. *Temperament in Clinical Practice*. New York: The Guilford Press, 1986.

Davis, Laura and Janis Keyser. *Becoming the Parent You Want to Be*. New York: Broadway Books, 1997.

de Marneffe, Daphne. *Maternal Desire*. New York: Little Brown and Company, 2004, 152–53.

Ehrenreich, Barbara and Arlie Hochschild. *Global Woman: Nannies, Maids, and Sex Workers in the New Economy*. New York: Henry Holt and Company, 2002.

Folbre, Nancy. *The Invisible Heart: Economics and Family Values*. New York: The New Press, 2001.

Hochschild, Arlie. *The Commercialization of Intimate Life*. Berkeley: University of California Press, 2003.

Hochschild, Arlie. *The Outsourced Self: What Happens When We Pay Others to Live Our Lives for Us*. New York: Henry Holt and Company, 2012.

Hochshild, Arlie. *The Second Shift*. New York: Viking Penguin, 1989.

Johnston, Kadija, and Charles Brinamen. *Mental Health Consultation in Child Care*. Washington, DC: Zero to Three, 2006.

Macdonald, Cameron. *Shadow Mothers: Nannies, Au Pairs, and the Micropolitics of Mothering*. Berkeley: University of California Press, 2010.

McLaughlin, Emma, and Nicola Kraus. *The Nanny Diaries: A Novel*. New York: St. Martin's Griffin, 2002.

Pawl, Jeree and Maria St. John. *How You Are Is as Important as What You Do*. Washington, DC: Zero to Three, 1998.

Purmal, Kate and Lisa Goldman. *The Moonshot Effect: Disrupting Business as Usual.* Wynnefield Business Press, 2016

Sandberg, Sheryl. *Lean In: Women, Work, and the Will to Lead.* New York: Random House, 2013.

Sandberg, Sheryl. "Why We Have Few Women Leaders," TED Talk, December 2010. https://www.ted.com/speakers/sheryl_sandberg

Scheftel, Susan. "Why Aren't We Curious about Nannies?" In *The Psychoanalytic Study of the Child* 66. New Haven, CT: Yale University Press, 2012.

Shonkoff, Jack. *The Science of Resilience.* Harvard Graduate School of Education, March 2015.

Slaughter, Anne-Marie. *Unfinished Business: Women Men Work Family.* New York: Penguin Random House, 2015.

Slaughter, Anne-Marie. "Why Women Still Can't Have It All." *The Atlantic,* July/August 2012. http://www.theatlantic.com/magazine/archive/2012/07/why-women-still-cant-have-it-all/309020/

Small, Meredith. *Our Babies, Ourselves: How Biology and Culture Shape the Way We Parent.* New York: Anchor Books, 1999.

Stern, Daniel N., M.D. *The Motherhood Constellation.* London: Karnac Books, Ltd., 112.

Stern. Daniel N., M.D., *The Birth of a Mother: How the Motherhood Experience Changes You Forever* New York: Basic Books, 1998.

Stout, Hilary. "How to Speak Nanny." *The New York Times*, February 3, 2010.

Winnicott, D. W. *The Child, the Family and the Outside World.* London: Penguin, 1973, 173.

Whitebook, Marcy, Caitlin McLean, and Lea Austin. The Early Childhood Workforce Index: State of the Early Childhood Workforce. Center for the Study of Child Care Employment, July 7, 2016.

TDaP (tetanus, diphtheria, and pertussis) vaccine, 101
telephone numbers, important, 230, 235
telephones, 97
tetanus, 101
training, 99, 164–65, 185–88
travel, 78, 97–98, 195–98
Travers, P. L., 27
trial period, 87, 129–30
trust, 32, 52–53, 166–67
TrustLine Registry, 100, 101
tuberculosis, 100–101
tutors, 77

V

vacations, 78, 94, 195–98
vaccinations, 101
values
    categories of, 61
    cultural, 64–65, 177
    definition of, 61
    importance of, 62
    interview questions about, 220
    learning, 61, 62
    LGBT families and, 152–53
    of parents vs. nannies, 62–66

    of respecting authority, 169, 178
    stereotypes and, 64
Van Dyke, Dick, 33
Vogelstein, Ahava, 186

W

Whitebook, Marcy, 182
whooping cough, 101
Williams, Robin, 136
Winnicott, D. W., 56
word of mouth, 116
working mothers
    challenges for, 22
    rise in number of, 17, 18, 20

Y

yo-yo effect, 46–47

ACKNOWLEDGMENTS

The Institute for Families and Nannies (TIFFAN) gratefully acknowledges the generous contribution from Alyce Desrosiers who donated this book to support TIFFAN's mission to provide professional development, education and training to nannies, research on quality of care and advocacy to professionalize the nanny industry.

From Alyce Desrosiers

When I began putting into words who and how others in my sphere of influence guided me through the process of writing this book, I felt stymied by the challenge. How could I give recognition and weight to the immense contribution others have made to the words on these pages? I quickly realized that as in any collective endeavor, everyone contributed a piece that couldn't stand alone yet was necessary for the whole.

My first and foremost recognition goes to my partner for the past 25 years, Michael Katz. Michael is a man of brilliant 'shorthand' summaries of thought and warm-hearted, deep foundational support. Never was there a doubt that he believed in the need for this book and the fundamental truth of the ideas it brought to life. His unwavering support of my ability to create and publish these ideas cannot be minimized.

My parents and eight siblings follow. My relationship with these most important people is woven into the fabric of this book. Throughout the formative years of our lives, my siblings and I tested and tried out the values of the Golden Rule, respect for authority and hard work. We depended on each other when the going got tough and learned that perseverance and hard work paid off in ways that went beyond monetary rewards. Honesty toward each other, coupled with not taking ourselves too seriously, took the rough edges off conflicts and squelched any sense of entitlement. We had little to go around, but we had each other. My mother passed away while this book was being written. She was proud to have a daughter who would carry on the traditions of her sister, my aunt, who wrote beautiful stories chronicling their family history.

My unwavering belief that relationships are the foundations of child development was laid down during my internship at The Infant-Parent Program (IPP) at the University of California San Francisco. It was the late 1980's, the beginnings of the research on infant-toddler development and of the importance of the infant-parent relationship in creating meaningful relationships with adults in later years. At the time, Kadija Johnston began the Preschool Consultation program at IPP. She sparked my interest in quality of care in childcare settings. Kadija subsequently went on to become the Director of IPP and has supported and consulted with me for the past 20 years as I've developed my work with parents, nannies and young children. She is my inspiration and role model. Other infant-parent clinicians from IPP who influenced my work greatly include Jeree Pawl, Steve Seligman, Maria St. John and Daphne de Marneffe. Others who have inspired my thinking include Marcy Whitebook for her unrelenting pursuit to ensure childcare professionals are paid a livable wage; Arlie Hochschild for her warmth and insight investigating how parents manage work and family; Cameron Macdonald and Susan Scheftel for giving nannies the recognition they needed to get out of the shadows and be visible; and Maureen Murphy, who steered me out of the fog to see more clearly what needed to be seen.

In late-2015 over lunch with my business mentor, Kate Purmal, a highly accomplished and heartfelt businesswoman, I disclosed my vision of starting a nonprofit agency to give nannies opportunities for continued education, training, career development and advocacy. Two years later, this book is published and the nonprofit established. Kate made this happen. She believed in the book and in the nonprofit and she believed in me. She has the knowledge and business acumen to make things happen efficiently and with success. I can never express enough my deep appreciation for Kate's support in making my dreams become a reality.

Every dream needs management by skilled artisans to be created. I have tremendous respect for the technical and artistic skills among those who massaged the book content into an art form. Karla Olson from BookStudio LLC shepherded the book through the start-to-finish maze of publication. She introduced me to others equal in expertise: Elaine Cummings and Lisa Wolff for editing, Tricia Hedman for public relations. Others came to me through various paths: Leslie Patrick, who contributed her own ideas and editing to the material; Torre DeRoche for her excellent graphic design and layout.

Day in and day out, and over the years, there have been those loyal and bright minds that knew where I needed support to be the best I could be: Ahava Vogelstein, my teaching assistant, parent educator and a former nanny; Lauren Sharpe, a vibrant children's art teacher and a former nanny; Kristen Davis, a thoughtful and soulful teacher and a nanny; Glinda Messina, a positive caring and giving nanny and auntie to many; Kathy Halland, a "got your back" loyal friend and bookkeeper, and Paula Bennet, a successful entrepreneur and warm-hearted colleague who believes small businesses loom large.

Kellie Geres, Marcia Hall and Sue Downey at The International Nanny Association (INA), Lora Brawley at Nanny Care Hub contributed their passion and dedication to the ideas in this book. Lyn Peterson at PFC Services has contributed her in-depth knowledge and street smarts to ensure parents get reliable background check reporting on nannies. The cohort of agency owners at The Association of Premier Nanny Agencies constantly strive to give families the best nannies available. Tom and Stephanie Breedlove of My HomePay and Kathy Webb of HomeWork Solutions, Inc. laid the foundation for families to know about and comply with the nanny tax. These dedicated professionals and many others are to be commended for their never-ending belief in nannies as professionals and their unequivocal, timeless support to professionalize the industry. I have drawn on their dedication, knowledge and support over the years.

None of this could happen without the parents who invite me into their living rooms and into their family lives to go through a process with them to make one of the most important parenting decisions they can make. The hundreds of parents and their children that I've created relationships with form the basis for this book. Collaborating with these families has expanded my worldview of what makes a family and a parent; of how children are raised and cared for; of resiliency, perseverance, creativity, connection and joy.

Then there are the thousands of nannies I've met along the way in coffee shops, libraries, playgrounds, Skype meetings and in the living rooms of parents. I've been humbled by the complexities of their personal lives, by their dedication to their work, by the love and care they give to other people's children. They are truly the group that has taught me so much about giving and caring while also walking in the shadows along the periphery of the childcare industry. In some small but important way, I hope this book sheds light on them—and the relationships they create with parents and the children they care for as well as the abiding value they provide.

CPSIA information can be obtained
at www.ICGtesting.com
Printed in the USA
FSOW02n2234080118
43188FS